BEING
CATHOLIC

How We
Believe,
Practice
and
Think

ARCHBISHOP DANIEL E. PILARCZYK

ST. ANTHONY MESSENGER PRESS
Cincinnati, Ohio

Scripture citations are taken from the *New American Bible with Revised New Testament and Psalms,* copyright ©1991, 1986, 1970 by the Confraternity of Christian Doctrine, Inc., Washington, D.C. Used with permission. All rights reserved. No portion of the *New American Bible* may be reprinted without permission in writing from the copyright owner.

Cover and book design by Mark Sullivan
Cover photo by Gene Plaisted, O.S.C.

LIBRARY OF CONGRESS CATALOGING-IN-PUBLICATION DATA

Pilarczyk, Daniel E.
  Being Catholic : how we believe, practice, and think / Daniel E. Pilarczyk.
    p. cm.
  ISBN 0-86716-708-4 (pbk. : alk. paper) 1. Catholic Church—Doctrines. 2. Spiritual life—Catholic Church. I. Pilarczyk, Daniel E. Believing Catholic. II. Pilarczyk, Daniel E. Practicing Catholic. III. Pilarczyk, Daniel E. Thinking Catholic. IV. Title.

BX1754.P528 2006
282—dc22

                                                                    2005024632

ISBN-13 978-0-86716-708-5
ISBN-10 0-86716-708-4

Published by St. Anthony Messenger Press
28 W. Liberty St.
Cincinnati, OH 45202
www.AmericanCatholic.org
www.SAMPBooks.org

Printed in the United States of America.

Printed on acid-free paper.

12 13 14 15   6 5 4

CONTENTS

INTRODUCTION

Professing the Catholic faith—being Catholic—is a rich and complex thing. People who have been Catholics all their lives still find themselves discovering new depths in their faith, and people who become Catholic in adulthood often find themselves moving into a new world in which things previously familiar take on a whole new light and meaning.

Those who profess the Catholic faith have a particular mindset, which I like to call "thinking Catholic." It is a mindset that includes attitudes about the world, about the people around them, about possessions, prayer and spiritual maturity that all grow out of their faith and color the way they think. Part of being Catholic is having a Catholic mindset.

There are also specific religious behaviors ("practicing Catholic") that arise from Catholic faith and tradition and which, taken together, constitute a way of being religious in an authentically and consciously Catholic fashion. Catholics go to Mass on Sunday and "get married in the church" and are devoted to Mary and the saints. They carry out a whole lifetime agenda of Catholic practices.

The bedrock on which Catholic thinking and Catholic practice rest, however, is the Catholic faith itself. This faith is not a matter of Catholics putting together for themselves some selection of generic beliefs but of "believing Catholic," of believing as the church believes, of believing as Christ taught. The belief of Catholics is not a set of beliefs that Catholics construct, but a sharing in the life of Christ that they receive.

Some time ago, I prepared three series of articles for the newspaper of the Archdiocese of Cincinnati, *The Catholic Telegraph*. These sets of short articles were entitled *Thinking Catholic*, *Practicing Catholic* and *Believing Catholic*. As each set of articles reached its conclusion in the newspaper, it was published in book form (with the same titles) by St. Anthony Messenger Press. Now these three small books are being gathered into one publication entitled *Being Catholic: How We Believe, Practice and Think*. The articles have been reviewed and revised, and, where appropriate, some references to the *Catechism of the Catholic Church* have been added to provide more detailed resources and suggestions for further reading.

The purpose of this book is to provide an overview of these three main aspects of Catholic faith and life. It intends to give some idea of the richness, complexity and vitality that are involved in being Catholic. It is addressed to persons who are already Catholic with the hope that it will enliven and deepen their Catholic faith and practice. It is also addressed to persons who are not yet Catholic with the hope that it will provide them with some sense of the variety and joy and depth of life that come with being Catholic.

This book is not intended to be an academic exercise. It is rather an act of witnessing, a testimony to the generosity of God that Catholics experience in accepting and living out the gift of faith that Christ has bestowed on them.

PART ONE
BELIEVING CATHOLIC

INTRODUCTION

Sometimes the Catholic faith seems frighteningly complex, even to Catholics. There's so much there! In fact, the *Catechism of the Catholic Church* that Pope John Paul II issued in 1992 as "a sure norm for teaching the faith" runs to 688 pages of text. This really isn't surprising when you consider that the Catholic faith deals with everything from before creation to the final fulfillment of redemption at the end of time, and has been the object of reflection and prayer and teaching for two thousand years.

Yet "believing Catholic" doesn't require a lifetime of professional study before one can begin. Fundamentally, believing Catholic is a matter of knowing and understanding and responding to a story, not a fictional story but the true story of God's love for us human creatures. That story provides the foundation on which all the ramifications of thinking Catholic and practicing Catholic are based, the framework that supports and structures all the 688 pages of the *Catechism*.

The purpose of this part of *Being Catholic* is to set forth the story. It's not meant to give each and every element of the Catholic faith or answer every question. It is meant to offer the essentials of believing Catholic, the fundamentals that have to be there if thinking Catholic and practicing Catholic are going to have any appeal or make any sense.

I hope that reading and reflecting on the story is as much of a blessing to the reader as the writing of it has been to the writer who, after seven decades, is still finding new reasons to be grateful for the gift of believing Catholic.

CHAPTER ONE

FAITH

Saying "We Believe"

What does it mean to believe? For one thing, belief means to accept something as true, whether or not we can personally demonstrate its truth. I believe that the planet Mars has polar icecaps and that the Battle of Waterloo took place in 1815. Most information we use in life is composed of this kind of belief. If we relied only on what we could prove personally or only on what we have personally experienced, we could rely on very little.

We Catholics hold certain beliefs about God and religion. We believe that there are three persons in God, that Jesus Christ is both divine and human, that there are seven sacraments, that the pope is head of the church. We accept these statements as true, even if we can't prove them scientifically, even if we're not sure of their full meaning.

But believing can be something far more profound than merely accepting a statement as true. Believing also means being a believer. It means having faith. Having faith does involve accepting truths, but, more deeply, having faith means giving ourselves over to a person and becoming part of that person's story. Religious belief concerns not just a body of truths but a person. Catholic Christian believing, sharing the Catholic faith, means voluntarily becoming part of the story of God's love for the world, becoming part of the story of the life and destiny of God's Son, Jesus. Our faith provides the only scenario that addresses the deepest dimensions of our lives. If we refuse our part in God's story, our lives lose their center and degenerate into meaninglessness.

The story to which we give our lives in faith is a single story. It is based on facts and truths that come together to make a coherent whole stretching from the moment of creation to the last instant of time, and into eternity. It is a love story about God's love for us and about the way God invites us to respond. It is a story in which each of us has an important part, a part that can be played by no one else. It is a story of success and failure, of generosity and sin, of clarity and confusion. It is a story about charity and justice. It is a story that is filled with meaning for each individual human being and for all of us together.

Being a believer, having faith, implies taking God at his word, accepting as true God's offer of love and concern for us, living out that acceptance in every aspect of our lives; not just with our minds, important as that is, but also with our hearts and our lives, with our jobs and our friendships, in times of deep reflection and in the humdrum moments that compose most of our life.

Accepting the truths and giving ourselves to the story are both important. A member of the church is expected to accept what the church believes and teaches. The believer is a person who can recite with honesty and sincerity that compendium of truths which the community prays at the Sunday liturgy and which we call the creed: "We/I believe…"

But being a church member is much more than just accepting that list of truths. Being a member of the church means handing ourselves over to the Lord who stands behind the creed. "Accepting as true" without personal commitment to what the truths imply turns the truths of faith into mere information.

Evelyn Waugh's novel *Brideshead Revisited* has a wonderful passage in which Rex Mottram, a superficial social climber, is taking instructions to become a Catholic so he can marry an heiress. He just wants to know what he has to believe so he can sign on the dotted line. Things go pretty well until the heiress's little sister mischievously tells Rex that Catholics believe that you have to sleep with your feet pointing east so that if you die during the night you can walk to heaven. He's ready to believe that, too, but he wonders why nobody told him before. Poor Rex! He was ready to sign on to a list of "truths" but not to engage himself in real faith. He was ready to "believe" but not to be a believer.

On the other hand, committing ourselves to a faith that does not have clear and specific teachings is an exercise in emotionalism. Both aspects of belief are important. Accepting the truths of the creed constitutes the bones and muscles of faith, but committing ourselves to what the truths mean is the heart and soul of faith.

Handing ourselves over to God with the intent to play our part in God's love story for our world and our life is not necessarily easy. Generally, the world around us neither welcomes religious belief nor regards it as important. Gestures are made at Christmas and Easter, but mostly our culture tells us that real importance lies in scientific knowledge and technology, success and wealth, prominence, looking out for oneself, avoiding pain and providing for ourselves the maximum amount of comfort and pleasure. Not all of these things are bad, of course, but in God's love story they are all secondary themes. They are not the main plot. Yet our society, our culture, tells us that it is faith that is secondary, that religious belief is a nice thing for those who find it helpful, but that the real world lies elsewhere.

Believing Catholic is hard because so many voices on the stage where God's story is being played out keep saying that it is basically irrelevant.

A while back, a twenty-story office building was constructed next door to the church complex where I live. Now our church building is overshadowed by the office building. Those two buildings symbolize faith and the world. What used to be a highly visible church now seems insignificant, as if the world were trying to cut faith in God down to size.

Still other factors contribute to making belief difficult, factors within ourselves. Sometimes our life seems so heavy, so confused, so meaningless, so sinful that we find ourselves wondering how God can really love us. Sometimes we wonder if the truths that underpin our commitment to the Lord are real. Did God create the world? Is Jesus God? Is the church actually part of God's story? Does an eternity of happiness await us?

More often than not, such questioning and confusion offer an opportunity for growth in our faith life. After all, faith does not consist in placidly accepting a body of self-evident statements that remain obvious and clear forever. Religious faith is not a geometry theorem or a cold historical fact. Religious faith is a personal relationship, a love affair between ourselves and the Lord, a love affair between ourselves and those the Lord loves. Every personal relationship implies growth. We change as our lives progress. Things once important seem less so at another time. Things once clear cloud over as our circumstances change.

As our relationship with God deepens and develops, we face challenges within ourselves, challenges to our selfishness and superficiality. Just when we think we have figured out our part in the story, we find aspects that don't seem to fit in. New approaches and new emphases are called for. This can be devastating if it leads us to give up our part in God's love story. But growth and maturity will result from our struggle if we hold on to our relationship with the Lord and weather the storm in the company of Jesus and his church. The struggle to understand and to accept is part of the life of faith, part of believing Catholic.

This book offers neither an exhaustive account of Catholic belief nor a simple list of truths that we are expected to accept if we would be Catholics. Its purpose is to outline the story in which we are all invited to take part, a story about creation and sin, about Jesus and the church, about grace and glory, about God and about us. The story is composed of truths—not truths for their own sakes, but truths as foundations for faith, for our participation in God's story. To take seriously our part in the love story that God has written for our life and for our world is the commitment we make when we give ourselves over to believing Catholic, when we say, "We believe."

For Discussion and Reflection

• *What elements in the world around you make it difficult for you to be a believer?*

• *When have questions or confusion about your faith led to personal growth?*

• *In what ways does your faith challenge you?*

From the *Catechism of the Catholic Church*

Nos. 144–167.

CHAPTER TWO

CREATION

The Masterpiece

"Marley was dead to begin with.... This must be distinctly understood, or nothing wonderful can come of the story I am going to relate." These words begin Charles Dickens's *A Christmas Carol* and are appropriate as we begin to reflect on the love story between God and the world, God and us human creatures, a story in which each of us has a part. You have to know the beginning if you want to understand the story.

God's love story begins with time itself, a beginning recounted in the first chapter of Genesis: "In the beginning . . . God created the heavens and the earth" (1:1). The account goes on to tell how God created light and the sky and the earth, vegetation, the stars, the animals. Finally, God creates human beings, male and female, giving them charge over all the earth. Then "God looked at everything he had made, and he found it very good" (1:31).

This beginning of God's love story has two main points: (1) the world was created by God, and (2) it was good.

Creation (and this includes the whole universe, not just the planet Earth) did not happen by chance. Creation was not a casual coming together of cosmic gases but a purposeful project undertaken by an infinite intelligence. Whether God at the beginning created everything exactly as we know it today (which seems unlikely), or whether God created a process which would evolve in time according to God's purpose is a secondary question. The main point is that our universe and our world are the result of God's will, an intelligent will, a free will, a will acting with a purpose, the will of the all-powerful and all-loving God.

The Genesis account makes clear God's role as creator; but it also tells us that the world God created was and is good. In the history of human thought, some have looked on the world as fundamentally bad, the product of the powers of evil, something to be tolerated, something to be rejected. Even today, some can see nothing of the world's beauty, nothing of its wonder but only pain, confusion and despair. Such an attitude is simply not in accord with believing Catholic.

At the same time, this good world is not God. Sometimes people are so entranced with the beauty, the power and the variety of creation that they see no need to look for anything beyond it, and so make the world into God. This is not correct either. Although the world reflects the goodness, richness and creativity of God, the world is distinct from God, different from God and not nearly good enough to be God.

What we have in the world, then, is a work of God's will, a work freely undertaken, which is distinct and different from God yet not opposed to God or separated from God.

Among the creatures inhabiting God's good world, the most important is the human creature. Genesis tells us that God made the human creature to reflect its creator differently than other creatures would. "God created man in his image; / in the divine image he created him; / male and female he created them" (1:27). Here we see the human part in the story that God was beginning to compose, a part greater than that of other creatures. Genesis makes clear that a human is not just one more animal.

We also see that human beings are essentially communal, not meant to be solitary. Men and women were created to work and act together.

What does all this say to us, millions or billions of years after God created the heavens and the earth?

For one thing, it tells us to celebrate creation, to enjoy it. Although the world is not our final goal, neither are we confined here as a punishment. The world is the product of the loving will of a loving God who has left traces of love everywhere to remind us of our origin and our destiny.

The world has its problems, of course. We shall see more about that later. Sometimes the problems seem so great that the term "world" is used, in Scripture and elsewhere, as a synonym for everything opposed to God. However, the basic truth remains that the world is good because it was made good by the good God who was beginning a love story that would go on forever.

Those who examine the world, rejoicing in its complexity and beauty, help us grasp these truths more firmly.

For example, there are the scientists, some of whom research the smallest building blocks of created reality while others look toward a seemingly endless series of stars. Some catalogue the thousands of species of animals and plants that have never been described before. In the human body, fundamental actions and processes are just now being discovered, while others remain for future generations to learn about and wonder at. There seems to be no end of natural phenomena that God has placed in the world, partly to keep its unimaginable complexity in careful balance and partly, perhaps, simply to express joy in the act of creating. We can almost imagine God saying, "Let's make a few more species of animals! Let's create another galaxy or two! It's good! It's very good!"

Artists describe the beauty of creation so that the rest of us can enjoy and appreciate it even more. They have been given the gift to see and make others see what might otherwise be taken for granted: the splendor of a wildflower, the brilliance of a bowl of fruit, the depth of meaning in a human face, the majesty of a human figure. We speak of artists as creative. More exactly, they reflect the creative genius of the good God who has created a good world, a world so permeated with good that much of its beauty would never be appreciated if it were not called to our attention.

Some artists work in words. They describe the complexities of human relationships. They point out to us the tragedies and the comedies of human existence. Every great novel somehow comments on the creation of humankind in the image of God, and every great poem comments on what God saw when he first looked on creation.

Teachers spend their lives helping others to know and remember what past generations have learned about the world, what past generations have done in the world. In the last analysis, every good teacher leads students to understand and appreciate the worth and the goodness of creation.

But God's creative power and the goodness of the world say still more to us. They tell us that the world is not a plaything with which to amuse ourselves and then cast aside. The world resulted from God's creative love and reminds us of that creative love. It is meant to be taken seriously. For that reason, we are called to respect creation. Creation is ours to use, but it remains God's to own. This truth has a particular urgency at a time when we have discovered ways to make the world uninhabitable through our abuses of water and air and food, not to mention our apparent capacity to destroy it completely with the weapons we have contrived.

Respect for God's creatures has a special meaning in our dealings with other men and women. Every single human being is made in the image and likeness of God. Every single human being is unique. For those reasons, there is a certain inviolability, a sacredness about other human beings, which the rest of us are called to defend and foster. We are not free to kill other human beings, mistreat them, allow them to live in inhuman misery or despise them because of their race or nationality. Every human being has a privileged place in creation, and, as participants in the world, we are all called to defend that privileged place. We are called to love other human beings because we are called to love God, who loves everything that has been created.

The world in which we live comes from a loving God. The world in which we live is fundamentally and perennially good. We have to grasp these foundational truths if we are going to understand and accept the part that God calls us to play in the love story that is the story of the world. In the beginning, when God created the heavens and the earth, the stage was set on which that story was to be played out. It is a good setting for a good story.

For Discussion and Reflection

- *What aspects of creation do you find most appealing in the opening chapters of Genesis?*
- *Where do you see God's love in the world?*
- *In what ways do you show respect for God's creation?*

From the *Catechism of the Catholic Church*
Nos. 337–343.

CHAPTER THREE

CREATION

The Ongoing Story

God didn't create the world a long time ago and then walk away. God did not set the stage and then leave the theater. Creation is still going on today, and God is still involved in it.

The fact that the world is still here indicates that God's creative love continues to operate. The world subsists not out of its own power but out of God's love. If God tired of it or somehow became distracted and forgot about it, even for an instant, all creation would simply cease to be. The world around us is a sign that God is still saying, "Let there be light and sky and earth and vegetation and animals and human beings." The world continues because God's creative action continues.

We know the world developed in various stages. Geologists describe periods when most of the world's surface was covered with ice. Species of animals have come and gone. Dinosaurs are no longer with us, and today's horses and cows are of relatively recent origin. The world's climate has changed many times. Some formerly temperate parts of the world are now almost uninhabitable, and vice versa. All sorts of things have happened since the beginning. All sorts of things continue to happen. God's power is still at work in the world. God has not yet finished with creation.

But God's ongoing creative work is perhaps most obvious in the world's chief creature, humankind. When God gave the first human creatures dominion over the world, told them to cultivate it, God invited humankind to participate in the development of the world. God called men and women not just to use the world but also to collaborate in making it, to be its cocreators. God created and continues to create a world that has a history, primarily a human history.

Several important implications are inherent in God's creating a dynamic and changing world. One is that human beings have a responsibility not just to respect and reverence what God has created, but also to develop it, to use it in a way that takes advantage of all the wonders God has put in it and brings about new wonders. When we speak of human creativity, we are speaking about the gift of ingenuity that enables and compels us to play our part in carrying forward the creativity of God.

In carrying out this responsibility, human ingenuity discovered fire, iron, then steel; how to build wheeled vehicles moved by animals, then wheeled vehicles that move themselves, then vehicles that move through the sky. While exploring and enhancing the possibilities of creation, human ingenuity found a way to fly to the moon as a first step to exploring the outermost reaches of space.

But human participation in God's creativity is not limited to what we can do with inanimate elements. Human creativity also deals with the development of humanity itself. As the centuries passed, we humans learned how to express ourselves, how to share our deepest feelings with one another. We developed various patterns of living together: in wandering tribes, in villages and cities, and now in an increasingly unified global society. We have come to know and care for our bodies more effectively with the result that today we are healthier and more long-lived than our ancestors. We have taught ourselves to think with increasing complexity, so that we can now deal not just with the pursuit of the next meal, but also with the structure of the universe and even, in some way, with the very nature of God.

As we consider human participation in God's ongoing creation of the world, we should recall that responsibility for the world belongs to each and every one of us. We all have our parts to play. Some—heads of nations, great thinkers, distinguished scientists—seem to have lead roles, while the rest of us spend less time in the limelight. But in fact, we all depend on each other. If political leaders, philosophers and scientists worked all alone, nothing would happen.

Some—perhaps most—important happenings in creation are never in the limelight at all: parents' care for their children, the love of a married couple, the affection shared between friends, the charity of a saint. A little reflection on our individual histories reminds us of the effect that people have on one another. What we are today is due in large part to the way in which other men and women have affected our lives.

We do not always see how our life fits with other people's. We do not always realize the effect that we have on others. The ongoing process of human development is often too complex for that, both at the level of individual human lives and at the level of human history in general. But the reality is there. Simply because we are human beings, we are each and all called to share responsibility for God's world, particularly for the world of humanity. We are each and all called to participate in God's creative activity.

In all of this, we must remind ourselves that God, too, has an ongoing part to play in creation. God is not over there, doing his thing, watching disinterestedly, as we do our thing. On the contrary, God is working in and through us. God has created the life of each of us. God has a destiny in mind for each of us. God is interested in each of us. As we attempt to carry out our role in the world, God stands by us, nudging us now in one direction, now in another, inspiring us to do this or that, leading us to carry out the divine plan for us and for those around us and, indeed, for the whole of creation. We are all responsible agents in the development of creation, but we are also all instruments of the all-wise and all-loving God.

We call God's action in the lives of each of us "divine providence." If it were not for divine providence, our responsibility for creation, instead of being a glorious adventure, would be a crushing burden.

Sometimes even people of faith find it hard to see divine providence at work in their lives. "How can my life make any difference?" we ask. "How can God bring anything out of what I am doing here and now?" "How can my suffering do anybody any good?" We find ourselves asking questions like these because we tend to underestimate God's goodness and God's power. We tend to think of God as being about the same size as ourselves and working as we do. In fact, God is infinitely more than we are, and the God who has promised to be at work in our lives is the same all-powerful God who created the whole universe out of nothing and is still busy with it today.

The fundamental truth here is that we are all important, important to God and important to the story of God's world. Each human life has something to contribute to the ongoing process of creation. If we lose sight of this, we run the risk of falling into meaninglessness. We begin to think that we are insignificant, a grain of sand in a galaxy. We become paralyzed, because if we are insignificant and without any real meaning there is no reason for us to strive, no reason for us to extend ourselves, no reason for us to do anything. Our lives become what Henry David Thoreau called "lives of quiet desperation."

Many people in our world struggle this way. In fact, there was a whole school of philosophy that dealt with human existence in terms of *ennui*, boredom. One member of that school, Albert Camus, said that the only basic question of human life is the question of suicide.

What God offers us is much more than boredom and the question of suicide. God offers us a glorious world, a world filled with beauty and so complex that we will probably never exhaust its mysteries. Even more, God offers us a part to play in that world. God calls us to share in its creation, to help make it what it was destined to become from the beginning. Nobody else can play the part that God has written for each of us. Our part in the drama may gain little notice from the other participants in creation, but believing Catholic involves the conviction that the part we have been given to play is eternally important to God. Otherwise, we wouldn't be here.

For Discussion and Reflection

- *What things in your life are of great value yet not "in the limelight"?*
- *How are you aware of God's presence and activity in your life?*
- *How are the people around you important?*

From the *Catechism of the Catholic Church*

Nos. 356–361; 299–308.

CHAPTER FOUR

SIN

The Wrench in the Works

God's creation is good. God's plan for the development of creation is good. Ideally, then, we should be living in a world in which the creative love of God is gratefully accepted by everybody working together to bring the world to its ultimate fulfillment. The human story should be a story of collaboration in what God intended for creation from the beginning.

But it's not. If we simply look around us, we realize that something has gone wrong. We see people filled with hate. The most intimate human relationships turn into occasions for self-serving behavior and rejection. People seem driven to possess the world's goods in endless quantity, far beyond what they need or can ever use. Joyful collaboration with creation's Lord is lost in a blind pursuit of immediate satisfaction. The good of some becomes an occasion of gnawing envy for others. God's gifts are received as if by right and used as if their human possessors were in total charge of them. Humanity's basic relationship with God is turned into a burden or into a matter of indifference.

Disarray in God's creation is not limited to individuals. In social systems, whole groups of people are despised and deprived of their rights because of their race; in economic systems people live and die in misery; in political systems service to others is replaced by the domination of the weak on the part of those who are more powerful.

Something is wrong here, and that something is sin. There are many ways to define sin: as unhealthy pride, as inflated sense of our own importance, as the deliberate violation of God's law or rebellion against God's plan. Another way to think of sin is as irresponsibility, an unwillingness to play our part in God's plan of creation. In sin, the main character in God's story for the world, the human character, decides that the script offered by God isn't good enough and begins to ad-lib, to play a part different from that intended by the Author.

We are all infected with sin. Maybe our sins are not major acts of outrage, but they are part of our lives nonetheless: acts of unkindness, great or small, toward those around us; excessive use of food and drink; petty selfishness that keeps us from sharing with others what we have and what they need; indifference to our relationship with God expressed in thoughtless prayer or in irregular worship, or even in a total disregard of God. A common expression of sin is the inclination to believe that we have no sin, that our lives are basically without blame, that our sinful choices are not really bad at all, or, even worse, that there is no such thing as sin.

Our sins are personal, but they are also social. Because we are gifted with free will, we share responsibility for the world. We may not be accountable for the origins of our society's injustice and oppression and lack of care, but we are accountable if we allow these sinful situations to continue. Sin is not just individual personal behavior; it also exists in the systems for which we share responsibility.

Sin is personal, social—and pervasive. In act or in consequence it is everywhere. There is no untainted island to which we can flee if we would be free of contact with sin. Sin is not outside of us. Sin is rooted deeply in every human heart. We cannot flee from it because we cannot flee from ourselves.

But why do we sin? What makes us inclined to irresponsibility toward God's creation and toward our part in it? Why does wrong so often seem so right?

For one thing, we have an inborn tendency to fall short of our destiny. Somehow, we find ourselves instinctively selfish, instinctively irresponsible and instinctively lazy. We are born morally defective. God didn't make us that way. God does not short-circuit the plans so carefully made for creation. God doesn't work against himself. We who believe Catholic believe that this inborn inclination to sin is the result of human decision that somehow broke off the original loving relationship between humankind and God.

Like everything else in creation, sin had a beginning. That beginning left its imprint on everything that followed. We are born with an inclination to sin because we belong to a species that inclined itself to sin. That first decision, that beginning of sinfulness among humankind, which we all share, we call "original sin." This is what is described in the third chapter of the Book of Genesis.

To understand original sin properly, some things need to be clear. One, original sin in us is not a sinful act for which we are personally responsible and for which we will be punished. Original sin is not something that we committed before our birth. Nor does God punish one person for the sins of another. Rather, original sin is a congenital, spiritual deficiency within us, a weakening of our ability to relate with God. Original sin, as applied to us, is a condition and not an action.

The church's teaching about original sin is not exclusively bad news, however. At least we know something about it. If we did not know about original sin, it would be impossible for us to understand how or why so much sinfulness exists in the world. Likewise, if we did not know about original sin, we would have to conclude that each of us is born morally perfect, with full potential to live a sinless life and that, if we do not live up to that potential, the blame is ours alone. Given who and what we are, we are simply unable to live totally sinless lives or to expect a totally sinless world. Knowing about original sin makes us realistic about ourselves.

Original sin, that first turning away from responsibility in God's plan, is not the only reason why we sin, however. We also are taught to sin. From our earliest moments we are in touch with people who are sinners. We unconsciously absorb sinful attitudes about love and hate, about wealth, about ambition, about self-sufficiency. No one sets out to make us bad, but we cannot help absorbing something from the world around us as we become aware of it. As our life develops, we consciously experience people who do wrong but are apparently successful and happy. Over and over again, we notice how attractive the short-term satisfaction of sin seems. Over and over again, we are shown the ways to get around our responsibilities as agents and instruments of God's plan for creation. It is not that everybody around us is trying to enlist us in a conspiracy of sinfulness; rather, sin is so pervasive that we cannot help being influenced by it.

We also sin as a result of our own past sins. Every time we go off on our own way, every time we shirk our responsibility as God's agents in the world, sin becomes easier the next time. Sin has deep roots, and once the plant begins to grow it is not easy to get rid of.

Two more things should be noted about sin.

First, pervasive and infective as it is, sin remains a secondary element in God's good world. The world remains what God made it, a reflection of God's own goodness and beauty. It is still basically good, despite all the misuse and irresponsibility that humankind has inflicted on it. Consequently, as we consider the sinfulness of the world, the appropriate response is not despair but hope.

Second, God has not abandoned the world. Despite that first rejection of God's plan, a rejection that still affects each of us, and despite the contribution that each of us had made and continues to make to the misdirecting of God's story line for creation, God is with us still. In fact, God is with us in ways that seem to surpass the original plan. Even taking sin into account, the story continues to unfold, and in many ways it is a better story than before, as we shall see.

With sin, humankind threw a monkey wrench in the works of God. But God is loving and powerful enough to keep the works going in spite of the wrench, indeed to make them work better.

For Discussion and Reflection

- *Why are people inclined to think of themselves as having no sin or even to deny that there is such a thing as sin?* Pride
- *What evidence have you seen that sin is rooted deeply in the world and in every human being?* Abortion, materialism
- *How can those who believe in original sin be people of hope?*

From the *Catechism of the Catholic Church*

Nos. 309–311; 386–390.

CHAPTER FIVE

JESUS OF NAZARETH
God's Gift

God's response to the irresponsibility of the human creature was not to turn away. God did not leave us to our own devices. Instead of abandoning us to our own sinfulness God sent us Jesus. In this chapter, we shall deal with the earthly life of Jesus. In the chapters that follow, we shall deal with the results and the significance of that life.

Jesus was God's gift to sinful humanity, but Jesus did not appear as some strange visitor from outer space come to sort everything out for us in spite of ourselves. Rather, Jesus was a human being who lived a human life in the midst of human beings, who carried out his mission in human categories. Therein lies the real significance of Jesus' life. To overlook or downplay the humanity of Jesus runs the risk of making him incomprehensible.

Jesus was born and grew up in backwater towns. He spent his life in an obscure country. He took part in the religious life of his people and his time. He was not a world figure while he lived. In many ways he seemed pretty ordinary. He learned, as we humans do, a little bit at a time. He experienced fear and anger and failure and disappointment. He was tempted, as we are, to turn aside from his human responsibility toward God.

Jesus' work during his time in the world was that of a Jewish religious teacher. To all who would listen he spoke about the love of God for us and about our love for God. He taught that God loves us more than we can imagine. He taught that God loves us all, sinners though we are, Jews and non-Jews alike. Jesus opposed the idea that God is merely a lawgiver and that our duty is to observe God's law in order to claim God's attention. God is much more than that. We are much more than that. Jesus taught his followers to look on God as an extravagantly loving father. He himself called God "Abba," or "Dad," and found peace and energy in the long periods of time he spent in prayer.

Jesus had harsh words for the religious leaders of his time who claimed worth on the basis of their own presumed righteousness rather than on the basis of God's generosity, and who were ever ready to accuse others of sinfulness and religious impurity. He had no time at all for hypocrisy and was eloquent in his criticism of those who would make our relationship with God into a burden.

The center of Jesus' teaching was the kingdom of God. He spoke of a whole new relationship between God and humankind in which sin would be destroyed, in which all pain and suffering would be transformed, in which God's blessings would be shared by everybody, in which we would enjoy an unimaginable new intimacy with God. As he worked miracles, giving sight to the blind and hearing to the deaf, even raising dead people back to life, Jesus taught that the kingdom had already begun, in him. Jesus also offered forgiveness to sinners. All this was to serve as a sign that something wonderful and new was at hand, that God's creation was entering a new phase.

Another important aspect of Jesus' life and teaching was his friends. He loved people, all sorts of people: women, children, men. His closest associates were those we call his apostles. They were not intellectual giants or socially important people but a group of men that included some small-time fish merchants, an internal revenue agent and one or two who might be suspected of political radicalism. They were ordinary men, not particularly bright and, as it turned out, not particularly courageous. But Jesus loved them and enjoyed being in their company.

Jesus was friendly with other people, too, people who were not always seen as particularly respectable. He seemed to have a special fondness for spending time with men and women who were rejects in the religious society of his time: people who made no secret of their sinfulness, men and women who were free and easy about the observance of religious ritual, those who collaborated with the Roman overlords and so had put themselves beyond the pale of Jewish acceptability. Nobody was too bad or too outrageous for Jesus to notice and love. This was a real scandal to those who exercised regular religious leadership. How could Jesus claim credibility if he kept giving attention to sinful men and women like that?

In what Jesus taught and did people found a new hope and a new freedom. If God's love is as abundant as Jesus said, if every human creature, even the seemingly unimportant, has a special dignity, if all are called to participate in the kingdom of God which has already begun, then Jesus was presenting a whole new world. People no longer needed to be ashamed of themselves, to feel the oppression of not really belonging or the despair of not knowing where to turn in their sinfulness. True, there was still sin in the world, there were still injustices to be dealt with, there was still the hypocrisy of the self-righteous to be healed, but the kingdom that Jesus preached put all this into a new perspective. What he was proclaiming and practicing was nothing less than a revolution—not the revolution of the terrorist or the political activist but a revolution of one who spoke for God, a revolution which would reorient the whole of creation.

That's why they killed him. The life and teaching of Jesus seemed so radical, so dangerous to the religious and civil authorities that they arranged to have him executed on false charges. Jesus was put to death as a criminal.

The death of Jesus was not just an injustice, not just the brutal termination of one more human life. The death of Jesus was a real act of witness. He was put to death precisely because of what he had taught and done. He was a martyr to his own lifestyle, to his own teaching. If he had been willing to compromise, to tone down what he was saying, to tell the people that they had misunderstood him, he might have saved himself from death on the cross. After all, the attack on him from the leaders of the people did not come as a surprise. Jesus saw it coming for a long time. Yet he remained faithful to his calling, faithful to his teaching mission, faithful to what he knew God expected from his human life.

Jesus was a human being who lived a human life like ours, a life that began with birth, that evolved through a certain number of years and that ended with death. That fact is essential to the meaning of his story.

But from another perspective, Jesus' human life was quite different from ours. To a greater or lesser extent, we live in selfishness and sin. We often try to turn creation in a direction other than God's. We overlook our responsibility to develop humanity into what God meant it to be, and instead settle for immediate personal satisfaction. When we look at our world, all too often we see not the handiwork of a loving God in which we are called to collaborate but a collection of opportunities for us to exploit. When we look at God, all too often we see not the infinitely loving God that Jesus called Father but the stern Lawgiver or the irrelevant Architect. When we look at our brothers and sisters in humanity, all too often we see not creatures of priceless dignity but tiresome men and women who seem called to make our life uninteresting and difficult.

Jesus' life was different. Yet its significance does not lie just in his sinlessness—although that is an important aspect of it—but rather in the fact that Jesus' life was what God had meant human life to be from the beginning. Here at last was one who understood the glory and love of God, a glory and a love reflected in creation, yet reaching far beyond the visible world. Here at last was one who collaborated in God's plan for the development and destiny of the world by bringing men and women to appreciate their dignity, by calling them to love one another, by teaching them the worth of even the most seemingly insignificant of their brothers and sisters, by making them aware of the depth and intensity of God's love for them. The priorities, categories, goals and values that Jesus exemplified in his life are those that God intended all human beings to live by when we were first created.

To say that Jesus lived a human life is absolutely correct and theologically precise. But in view of the significance of that life in the story of ongoing creation and in the story of God's human creatures, we could also say that Jesus lived not just *a* human life but *the* human life, *the* human life *par excellence*.

But all this is only the beginning. There are other facets of the reality of Jesus still more wonderful, still more significant. His life and his mission did not end with the cross. In a way, they only began there.

For Discussion and Reflection

• *What aspects of Jesus' life are most appealing to you?*

• *What aspects of Jesus' life are most puzzling to you?*

• *What implications does Jesus' association with the "rejects" of his society have for a Christian believer today?*

From the *Catechism of the Catholic Church*

Nos. 456–463; 514–521.

CHAPTER SIX

RESURRECTION

The Fulfillment

If Jesus' life had ended on the cross, his story might have been a high point in creation. Here was someone who had done everything right, had followed God's plan for the world in his words and actions, had attempted to contribute to the development of what God had begun in the human creature, had apparently demonstrated how rich and how spiritually profound a human life could be. It was an exemplary life.

But Jesus' life ending on the cross would also have been one of the saddest stories in the history of creation. He who carried out God's will as none had done before would have died leaving only a memory behind, a memory of rejection and failure, a memory of a man done to death by the fear and narrowness of his fellow human creatures. If Jesus' life had ended on the cross, it would have been one more monument to the triumph of human irresponsibility, to the triumph of human blindness, to the triumph of sin. Everything would be the same as it was before, with Jesus as the great exception proving the rule of futility in human endeavor.

But Jesus' life did not end on the cross. Soon after he had died, he reappeared. He came back to his friends and followers. They recognized him as being the same Jesus they had known before, even though he was somehow different. His greeting to them was a greeting of peace. He calmed their fears at seeing him by assuring them that he was not a ghost. On many different occasions, he associated himself with them again when they were gathered to recall his memory, when they sat together at meals, even when they worked at their fishing business.

He continued to teach them. He explained to them how his life was the fulfillment of everything that God had planned for creation and humankind. He told them that they would soon receive his Holy Spirit and that they were to forgive sins even as he had. He pardoned them for their cowardice when they had run away from him, and said that he would be with them forever. Most important of all, Jesus told them that they were to carry his teaching about the kingdom of God throughout the whole world without fear, that his life was not to be an end but a beginning, the beginning of something that would last until the end of the world.

After a time the disciples did not experience him in the same way any more; but they knew that he was still active in their midst, because he promised that he would be and because they found in themselves courage and power and enthusiasm that had not been there before.

The significance of the resurrection of Jesus lies in what God says in and through it. In bringing Jesus gloriously back from death, God is saying that a life like the life of Jesus is too good to end, too important to be overcome by human sinfulness, too significant to be relegated to the realm of mere memory, too precious to be the one-time exception in the story of creation.

By raising the humanity of Jesus from the dead, God is giving a divine sign of approval of the quality and meaning of Jesus' life. God is saying, in effect, "The life of this man is what human existence is all about—love and friendship and compassion and faithfulness and self-sacrifice, total dedication to the divine plan for creation, total giving of the human self to the work of the Creator even if the short-term result is rejection and death. This is what I want human existence to be and I want it to be so gloriously and forever." The Resurrection is God's "Bravo!" for Jesus' part in the story of creation.

Finally, somebody had done it right! Jesus had played his part fully as written by the Author, and the Author wants Jesus' role in creation never to end. That's why the humanity and the life of Jesus did not come to a close with his death. It is still going on. It is still important to God. It is important for us.

To understand the resurrection of Jesus appropriately, we must realize, first of all, that Jesus' resurrection was a radical transformation. Jesus' followers knew that it was he whom they were seeing because they had known him so closely during his life. He still carried the marks of the nails in his hands and feet. He ate with them after the Resurrection as he had done before. He remembered them, who they were and what they had done. They were able to give witness that it was the same Jesus.

But Jesus was different, also. He walked through closed doors. He came and went at will, and appeared in unexpected ways. Even though he was the same Jesus, his friends did not always recognize him right away. He was the same Jesus, but he was not a revived corpse, come back from the dead to start living again in the same old way. He had been changed, transformed, glorified—still human but translated to a whole new level of being.

We have to be quite clear about Jesus' bodily resurrection. His body rose from the dead, the same body that it had been before. People who are indifferent about whether or not Jesus' body decayed in the tomb are missing one of the most important aspects of the Resurrection. The identity of the glorified Jesus after the Resurrection with the historical Jesus who had been put to death on the cross is supremely important because of what it says not just about Jesus and his life, but also about God's good creation and about God's plans for that creation.

The bodily resurrection of Jesus is a revelation about human life. Transforming Jesus and raising him from the dead is God's message about an unsuspected potential in created reality. In Jesus' new life, a life untrammeled by the constraints of space and time, we become aware that not all that exists is destined for decay. We come to understand that this world and God's plans for it hold greater depths than what we see. We learn that human life need not be destined for death and failure but for transformation and glory—not in some metaphorical way, as we might speak of a glorious memory, but really and truly. In the resurrection of Jesus the second act of creation begins, an act as real as the first but even more exciting.

The resurrection of Jesus, however, is a reality that can be perceived only by faith. Sometimes we find ourselves wondering how Jesus got out of the tomb. We wonder whether the soldiers tried to stop him as they saw him walking away. We wonder why Jesus didn't go to Annas and Caiphas and Pilate and rebuke them for their cruel injustice to him. But all of that is irrelevant to what the Resurrection is really about.

The resurrection of Jesus is not just one more event in the history of the world, not just one more set of circumstances subject to human inquiry. The resurrection of Jesus is *beyond* the categories of human history. No eyewitnesses saw Jesus step out of the tomb because the Resurrection was an act of God that carried Jesus beyond the ordinary human realms of time and space into a whole new kind of being. The only way to be in touch with the resurrection of Jesus is to be in touch with the realm of God through faith, to have handed ourselves over to God's realities, to have offered ourselves to play our part in God's story—a story in which the resurrection of Jesus is a major climax. That doesn't make the Resurrection any less real. It simply means that we cannot deal with it in the same way we deal with the material realities around us.

#3 ~ And yet the resurrected Jesus has witnesses. Those who have come in touch through faith with the reality of the Risen Christ in their own lives, those who have accepted the full reality of God's love as manifested in the life of Jesus are witnesses to his Resurrection just as the apostles were. The faith of each of us is a testimony to the power and reality of the Risen Christ. *We* are the witnesses to the life and power of Jesus, who is with us today as he was with the apostles on the first Easter.

Finally, we need to observe that the resurrection of Jesus was not just something nice that God did for one man at one point in time. In fact, the resurrection of Jesus is of fundamental and intimate importance to all creation, to each of us now. We shall explore that more fully as we reflect more on the reality of Jesus in our next chapter and then on the implications of the life and resurrection of Jesus in the chapters that follow.

For Discussion and Reflection
• *What do you think God is saying to you through the Resurrection?*
• *Is the resurrection of Jesus a source of hope to you?*
• *What does it mean to you to say that believers of today are witnesses to the reality and power of the Risen Christ?*

From the *Catechism of the Catholic Church*
Nos. 638–647; 651–655.

CHAPTER SEVEN

INCARNATION

The God-Man

After Jesus rose from the dead and then returned in his risen and glorified body to his Father, the Spirit came upon the apostles. These weak and cowardly men were changed into enthusiastic witnesses to the kingdom that Jesus had preached. But there was more to the coming of the Holy Spirit than an infusion of courage. The apostles not only began to behave differently; they also began to see things differently.

As the apostles reflected on the few brief and eventful years that they had spent in Jesus' company, they realized with increasing intensity that Jesus had been more than he seemed. They reflected on his miracles, on his forgiveness of people's sins, on his teaching that a person's final and eternal value would be judged by how that person had related to him, to Jesus. They reflected on the special meaning that he seemed to give to the phrase he liked to use in describing himself: "the Son of Man." He was often called "Lord," a word used to address God. Sometimes he allowed himself to be called "Son of God" and to be referred to as "the Christ," the promised savior.

Jesus' relationship with God seemed different from other people's. He seemed more familiar with God, more in tune with God. Jesus referred to God as "Abba" ("Dad"), which seemed to indicate that he enjoyed a relationship with God that others did not. Then came the Resurrection and glorification of Jesus. Was it merely a sign of approval from God for what Jesus had done and said during his public life, or was it a sign of something more?

As the apostles and the other followers of Jesus reflected on him under the guidance of the Holy Spirit, they became aware that Jesus was indeed more than he seemed. Jesus, full and complete human being, was at the same time no one less than God.

Jesus' followers taught about the story of his life, death and resurrection. They began to express, as best they could, the astounding truth of which they had become aware: that Jesus was God who had lived in their midst. Soon these accounts were written down by those who had heard the apostles, accounts that ultimately became the Gospels in the New Testament.

Then there was Paul. Paul may have known about Jesus and his earthly life, but he certainly didn't understand what Jesus was or what his life was all about until his revelation experience on the road to Damascus (see Acts 9:1–6). After that, Paul took his place with the other apostles. Paul's letters to various Christian groups form a large part of the New Testament. In these letters Paul speaks of Jesus as one who, although divine, did not cling selfishly to his equality with God but emptied himself to assume the condition of a slave (see Philippians 2:6–11). Paul described Jesus as "the image of the invisible God," who existed before anything was created, and who holds all things in unity. (See Colossians 1:15 ff.)

By the time the last parts of the New Testament were written, the divinity of Jesus had become ever clearer, so that we find the author of the Gospel according to John saying, "In the beginning was the Word...the Word was God...the Word became flesh and made his dwelling among us" (John 1, ff.).

The whole New Testament is a series of writings about Jesus who lived and died a fully human life, but a life through which he revealed himself to his followers as one truly divine. That was the message the apostles were sent to deliver and the message that has come to us.

But if Jesus was God, why didn't he just say so? Why didn't he come right out and tell the apostles so they could tell everybody else? Basically because it would have been too much for them to take. They knew God as totally other, unapproachable, awesome. Until they had experienced the full force of Jesus' life and teaching, they would have been overwhelmed with fear, incomprehension, or even outrage at the very idea that anything human could also be God. They needed to experience the warmth of Jesus' life, the power of his teaching, the tragedy of his death and the glory of his Resurrection as well as strengthening from his Spirit before they could even begin to understand.

Even then, they could only speak in halting words because there wasn't even a vocabulary to express what they had experienced. Believers would struggle for centuries to find a way to understand and to speak precisely about what it meant for Jesus to be both God and man.

Some said the human in Jesus was merely an appearance. Others said that Jesus' divinity was only God taking a human being to himself and making him a son by adoption. Still others said that the human and the divine were united in Jesus because the divinity of God took the place of the human soul of Jesus. The Arians contended that Jesus was *almost* God, a kind of semi-divinity who had charge of the world, but, in the last analysis, was only a creature. The Nestorians taught that in Jesus there existed two subjects—two entities, two persons—one human and one divine, who worked in harmony, and that the person of God dwelt in the human person of Jesus as in a kind of temple. Still another group, the Monophysites, thought that humanity and divinity were mixed together in Jesus in such a way that his humanity was really absorbed by his divinity.

These attempts to understand and express the reality of Jesus all failed because they didn't adequately account Jesus as really God, or because they didn't adequately account Jesus as really human, or because they separated divinity and humanity to the point that Jesus was not one being but two.

Conclusive theological formulation of the reality of Jesus came at the Council of Chalcedon, more than four hundred years after the apostles. The church solemnly defined that Jesus was (and is), in one and the same subject, perfect in divinity and perfect in humanity, and that his divinity and his humanity are united without mixture, without change, without division, without separation.

If we still do not grasp the fullness of Christ or the total significance of his story, at least we have the terminology for thinking and speaking about him and about the factors that must be preserved as we deal with Christ in faith.

Dividing up Christ is not something confined to church history books. Some people today refuse to believe that Jesus was divine. For them, he may be a great teacher or a splendid model of human behavior, but that's all. Others refuse to accept that Jesus was human. They think of his life as effortless, without the real pain and frustration that every human experiences. Both approaches are wrong; both are incomplete because neither accounts for the full reality of Christ.

If the Christ we reverence is not fully divine, if the Christ we worship is not fully human, if his humanity and his divinity are not united in a single subject, then the Christ we are dealing with is not the Christ of the apostles nor the Christ of the Christian faith, but a figment of our own imagination.

But what difference does it make? Granted that Jesus was a real human being, what does it add to say that he was God? Granted that he was God, why bother about whether he was really human? The Christian answer is crucial when it comes to considering our own relationship to God in redemption and grace and glory, when it comes to considering the community of believers that is the church, when it comes to figuring out what our own individual human existence ultimately means.

To say that Jesus is one being, both human and divine, is to say that in him God became a human actor on the stage of the world's history, that God became a human participant in the love story that had begun with creation. With God as a human participant, the story takes a whole new turn, and so does our part in it.

For Discussion and Reflection

• *Have you ever had trouble explaining deep things about yourself to somebody else?*

• *Have you ever had trouble understanding the full depth of someone else's personality?*

• *What difference would it make to you if Jesus were not God?*

From the *Catechism of the Catholic Church*
Nos. 124–127; 441–445; 464–469.

CHAPTER EIGHT

SALVATION
The Accomplishment

As we have dealt with believing Catholic, we have spoken about creation: God's good creation and God's plan for our collaboration in creation. We have spoken about sin, about the way in which we human creatures have misused and continue to misuse what God has given us, about how we have acted and continue to act irresponsibly in regard to what God has invited us to do in creation. We have spoken about Jesus, about his life and death, about how his life was the perfect human life, lived in the way in which God had meant all human life to be lived and how, therefore, Jesus was raised from the dead in glory as a sign of God's approval of his life. We have also spoken about Jesus as God, as the Son of the Father, fully human yet fully divine. Now it is time to say a little more about what Christ accomplished through his human existence and how that accomplishment fits into the story of God's creation.

As the God-Man, Jesus was not just one more human being. His life was not just one historic episode in God's creation. Jesus' human life was *the* human life *par excellence*, but if that's all it was, we would have been worse off than we were before—still struggling with our sins, but now looking with despair at the example of him who had done things right, but in a way that would have been beyond our imitating. Yet that's not how things are.

Our Catholic faith teaches us that, as the God-Man, Jesus lives more than human life. God is present to every time and place; therefore, the human life of Jesus, united to God without separation, becomes present to every time and place. But that's not all. Through the power of his divinity, all human life is transformed. The divine and human life of Jesus offers humankind a whole new way of being. Just as in Jesus God became human like us and took a human part in the story of creation, so also the life and death and resurrection of Jesus, divine and human, both invite and enable us to become like him—not just in his humanity but in his divinity as well. He makes his divine life available and accessible to us, so that we can live our human existence transformed by the power of his divine Spirit.

God was so taken with Jesus' life that he wanted every human creature to live the life of Jesus. When Jesus comes into our lives, God recreates us, reshaping our human qualities through the love of Jesus. Our human life becomes Jesus' life, human and divine.

This is *salvation*. This is what it means to say, "Jesus has saved us." In ordinary terms, saving is the opposite of throwing away. The criterion for saving or throwing away is worth or value. We save what is worth something to us; we throw away what is not. Saying that we are saved by Christ means that God makes us worth bothering about. Salvation makes us precious to God in an entirely new way because it makes us like Christ, both human and divine.

In addition to speaking of what Christ accomplished in his life as "salvation," the Christian tradition also speaks of it as "redemption." *Redemption* means being freed, being liberated from a situation of imprisonment or confinement. When we are redeemed by Christ, we are transported into a new context of freedom.

Because we become like God in Jesus, we enjoy freedom from sin. In our purely human existence, everything seems somehow to be mixed up with evil. When we are redeemed, we are assured that we need not be overcome by sin. The powers of sinfulness within us and around us will not have the last word because the life we live is no longer just a human life but the life of Christ, a life whose conclusion is not defeat but transformation.

Redemption also frees us from death. This does not mean that our earthly life will go on forever, but that our earthly death is only a stage on the road that leads to the full manifestation of what God has made us to be. For those who are saved or redeemed, suffering and death, real as they are, are not the final realities but a prelude to something far different and far better. Our life, like Christ's, is directed not toward death but toward resurrection.

Redemption also frees us from the law of achievement. In this world of ours, nothing is free. We each have to make our own way, and those who cannot are driven to the wall. But the life of Christ, which comes to us with salvation and redemption, is not something we earn. We cannot earn it because we cannot make ourselves worthy of something so far above us. We receive it as a gift of God or we receive it not at all. Once we live Christ's life, all merely human striving fades into relative insignificance. Even a life that seems to end in failure, like Jesus', is a life destined for glory, like Jesus'.

Once we share in Jesus' life, everything changes. We no longer need to suffer alienation or loneliness, to be enslaved by fear or despair or meaninglessness. Things that turn life into hell on earth for so many people can now be surpassed, transcended, transformed by the life of Christ that goes on in our life. Likewise our human accomplishments, those few things we have to be proud of—our acts of concern for others, our love for family and friends, our understanding and improvement of the world around us—all these are transformed and elevated because they are not just our accomplishments but also the accomplishments of the life of Christ who lives in us.

The life of Jesus, then, is not over. It goes on in his risen humanity, but also in us. Through his divine humanity, the life of Jesus has come into our life. We no longer live alone. We live with and in him.

What is true of us individually is true of the world as a whole. Thanks to the life, death and resurrection of Jesus, divine and human, our world is no longer merely the creation of God, good as that is. It is now the place where God's human and divine activity in Jesus continues to unfold. It is God's world in a way in which it was not before God became a human participant in it. It has been given a new direction and a new significance.

All this is what we mean when we say that Jesus saved and redeemed us.

Now perhaps we can see how fitting it was that Jesus was both human and divine. If Jesus had been merely a human being, his life would have been, at best, an example. On the other hand, if God had chosen to restore the world without the collaboration of humanity, the restoration of the world would have been an acknowledgment that things had gotten so bad that they could only be dealt with through an interruption from outside. By redeeming and saving the world through humanity, the humanity of Jesus, God indicates that the original plan was a good plan. God acknowledges the inherent worth of the human creature by using humanity to save and redeem humanity from ultimate failure. We have been saved and redeemed through the power of God, but we have also been saved and redeemed by a human being like ourselves. God has an ingenious way of doing things.

The life, death and resurrection of Jesus, therefore, were not just a flash in the pan, a kind of "time out" in the ongoing history of the misuse and mismanagement of God's good world. On the contrary, the saving and redeeming event that was Jesus' life was a whole new beginning for the world and its human creatures, a transformation of creation's direction and meaning. It constituted the beginning of the second act of the story of creation, an act whose finale will be the full and final assumption of the world into the glory of God in the Risen Christ at the end of time.

Many questions remain. How are we transformed by the salvation and redemption that Christ accomplished? What does it mean in practice for us to live the life of Christ? If Christ lives in us, how and why do we still sin? If the world is God's in a new way, thanks to the presence and activity of the Risen Christ, why is it still such a sorry place? These are urgent matters for believers, and their answers lie in what the Christian tradition calls grace.

For Discussion and Reflection

• *What does it mean to you to say, "Jesus has saved me"?*
• *In what ways do you see God's plan of salvation and redemption at work in the world?*
• *What difference has the life of Jesus made in your own life?*

From the *Catechism of the Catholic Church*
Nos. 619–623.

CHAPTER NINE

GRACE

The Sharing

In the Catholic Christian tradition, grace signifies Christ's life in us. In ordinary speech, *grace* means "charm" or "appeal" ("She is a very graceful person."), but the word's root meaning has overtones of kindness, favor and gift. In Christian belief, therefore, *grace* suggests God's goodness and generosity, which endow us with the life of Christ. Grace is gift *par excellence*.

Grace is our sharing in the salvation and redemption of humankind that was accomplished by the life, death and resurrection of the God-Man, Jesus. It is a new kind of relationship with God. When we are in the state or relationship of grace, we, as individuals, have been created again so that the life of Christ continues and evolves in our individual human existence. In a way that only God can bring about, we live Christ's life in our own.

It is important to realize that grace is a gift, freely given us by the Spirit of God. We cannot earn or deserve this relationship because we can have absolutely no right to it. Left to ourselves we would remain in constitutional sinfulness, muddling through as best we could, looking to God as something outside ourselves. But God does not leave us to ourselves. God comes to us on his own initiative and makes us over so that, in addition to being ourselves, we are also somehow participants in the life of Christ.

Yet we do have a part to play in grace. God does not make us sharers and participants in the life of Christ whether we want to be or not. God *offers* us the new life of Christ as a gift that we are invited to accept.

Moreover, grace is not just an individual relationship between God and us. Grace is offered to us through other human beings, through and in the community of those who believe in Christ, which we call the church.

All this comes together and is expressed in baptism. (Most often, we Catholics think of baptism as something for babies. In fact, baptism is primarily for adults. The baptism of infants is conferred in view of an adult relationship with God that exists in the church and in the child's sponsors and family and which will develop as the child assimilates personally what he or she was given at baptism.)

Presenting oneself for baptism expresses a willingness to share in the life of Christ, to be part of God's story for the world in and with Christ. The candidate for baptism expresses some level of faith. Through the ministry of the church in baptism, God transforms this incipient openness to Christ and establishes a new relationship between the candidate and Christ. (Note that even the candidate's preliminary faith is itself the gift of God and not something achieved for oneself.) God gifts the candidate with Christ's life. The candidate is precious to God in a whole new way. The candidate now shares not only the life of Christ, but also the lives of all others who live in Christ. We come into grace, then, and into the church, through God's gift of faith and baptism.

What does this mean in practice?

First of all, from God's perspective, the newly baptized person is no longer living merely as creature but is now someone living and continuing *the* human life *par excellence*, the life of Christ, the God-Man.

From our perspective, grace in practice is a matter of new meaning and new priorities. If we consciously and conscientiously live the life of Christ, our scale of values will be different from that of people who have not accepted Christ. Money, for example, will mean something different to us. So will success. So will friendship, marriage, work and leisure. So will sickness and death. All these things, and others, have a different meaning to those who live in Christ simply because Christ's life is a different life.

Moreover, living in grace precludes serious and deliberate sinning. The New Testament teaches clearly that we cannot live Christ's life and at the same time be murderers, thieves or slanderers. We cannot live the life of Christ and indulge ourselves in sexual irresponsibility, jealousy or quarreling. It is not that the relationship of grace makes us incapable of sinning. Our own experience teaches us that. Nor is it that God becomes angry with us when we sin and calls off the relationship between Christ and us. Rather, by seriously sinful conduct we make it impossible for Christ to live in us and, as it were, drive him out of our lives. Sinful behavior is incompatible with the life of grace; where sin exists the grace of Christ cannot be. This is easy to understand if we remember that another way to speak of grace is as holiness, the holiness of Christ.

If all this is true, how and why do people who are supposed to be believers, who are supposed to be living the life of Christ, behave the way they do? They all sin. If their life is the life of Christ, how can this be?

God does not overwhelm us with grace and make us do what we are supposed to do whether we like it or not. On the contrary, just as we must exercise our human freedom to *accept* the life of Christ in faith, so also we must exercise our human freedom to *assimilate* his life and carry it out in our lives.

God respects our freedom. God invites us to recommit ourselves to faith and to Christ over and over again, day by day, in a thousand human decisions and choices, big and small. Grace, the life of Christ, invites growth and development in the life of the individual. We can respond and grow ever stronger in Christ; we can neglect grace and grow indifferent; we can even reject it completely. The decision to accept our part in Christ's story is only the first of many, and it needs to be reaffirmed in every circumstance of our lives—not because God is ungenerous or wants to make things difficult, but because our human collaboration and response are important to God in the development of Christ's life in our midst. The exercise of freedom is an essential factor in Christ's ongoing life in grace in us just as it was in the earthly life of Jesus.

This also explains why the world is still so clogged with sin, selfishness and irresponsibility. Society and culture, the contexts in which we live, result from human decisions. Human decisions made the world the way it is and human decisions keep the world as it is. If, after the life of Christ has been unfolding on earth for twenty centuries, the world is still a mess, it is not because the life of Christ has been ineffective but because it has been so effectively rejected by generations of human beings (including Christian believers). Just as God does not force individuals to live out Christ's life consistently as individuals, so also God respects human freedom in the social and cultural context. The story of the world is the story of Christ's life, but also the story of human freedom.

A few more observations need to be made about grace if we are to avoid misunderstanding. First, grace is a spiritual gift, not a psychological experience. We don't necessarily perceive or feel grace. Feeling good about God no more proves the presence of grace than questioning or struggle indicate its absence.

Next, grace is more than God treating us *as if* we were like Christ. Grace is a real interior transformation that makes us infinitely different than we were before.

Finally, grace is not a bus ticket to heaven, an object or thing which God gives us and which we have to hang on to if we want to be saved. Grace is the life and holiness of Christ given to us by the Holy Spirit. It calls for response and development from us. We are called to live out the life of Christ, not merely to possess it.

Grace, then, is our participation in the salvation and redemption accomplished by Christ. Grace is the story of the life of Christ extended to all ages and all places. Grace is also our story, our part in his life, played out in our time and in our world in the company of all those who believe in him. And that brings us to our consideration of the church.

For Discussion and Reflection

• *What would your life be without baptism?*
• *Why do you think people sin even after they have received God's grace?*
• *How does your awareness of grace influence your attitudes and values?*

From the *Catechism of the Catholic Church*
Nos. 1996–2005.

CHAPTER TEN

CHURCH

The Community

Grace is the life of Christ, extended by the Holy Spirit into the lives of individual believers. Because there is only one Christ, all who accept Christ participate in one life. Consequently being in Christ through grace means being together with all others who are in Christ. This community of believers in Christ, established and held together by grace, is the church.

Our common life in Christ is a spiritual reality. We can't see grace or test for it as we test for radon. Nonetheless, the community of believers that is the church is more than a spiritual gathering. Just as Jesus' humanity was visible and palpable, so also his church is a visible organization, involved in the story of creation and redemption with its own earthly reality, its own history and its own particular activity. But because the church exists to carry out and continue the life of Christ, the activity of the church also reflects and expresses the activity of Christ.

Primarily the church brings Christ's holiness to its members. This is the meaning of its sacraments. In baptism, the "constitutional" sacrament, the church acts as the sign and agent of God in conferring the life of Christ on believers. Baptism both symbolizes and brings about the life of grace in the baptized person; at the same time, it makes the person a member of the community of those who share that life.

The other sacraments deepen and make explicit the life of Christ at various moments in the life of the believer, or consecrate the believer's life for particular service in the community. Thus, confirmation offers strength for living out the life of Christ in our human existence. The Eucharist nourishes us in the life of Christ. When we sin, the sacrament of reconciliation offers us forgiveness and renewed life in Christ. When we are seriously ill, the sacrament of anointing offers us courage to face our suffering in union with the life and suffering of Christ. Matrimony confers the holiness of Christ on the human relationship of love between woman and man and makes that relationship a context of grace for future generations. Holy orders establishes the deacon, priest or bishop in a position of special service to the life of Christ in the church.

All the sacraments are actions of the church. All the sacraments are the actions of Christ. All the sacraments are signs and instruments of the grace of Christ in the life of the believer and of the church.

As minister of holiness, the church also prays. In the liturgy, its corporate and formal worship, the whole community of believers offers praise and thanksgiving to God. There we all pray and Christ prays with us and in us. The worship we offer to God in the church is not just ours but his as well. It makes us holy because it is done with and in Christ.

As Christ taught, so also the church teaches. It presents and perpetuates the teaching of Christ. It reflects on the teachings of Christ and his apostles in order to understand their implications and applications for us now. Just as the sacraments are not the action of the church alone but of Christ as well, so also the teaching of the church is not just the thought of human believers, which we are free to accept or reject, but also the teaching of Christ himself. The church teaches with the authority of Christ because it is Christ who teaches in the church.

As Christ was a leader, so also the church leads. It provides direction for its members just as Christ did for his apostles. It calls them to express the holiness of the life of Christ in their own lives. It presents common modes of expression for prayer and faith. It calls its members to be aware that the community to which they belong is not just their local parish, but also a fellowship that extends throughout the world. It provides the laws and rules that are necessary in the life of any community composed of human beings.

Some in the church have been entrusted with a special call to leadership: the church's ordained ministers who, in different ways and to different degrees, are charged with expressing the church's teaching and guiding its worship. They are servants of the other members, called to help them live the life of Christ.

But the church is also a community composed of human beings, with all that that implies. For one thing, there is sin in the church. Its members are all still assimilating Christ's life; they are not perfect. That's why each church building has confessionals or reconciliation rooms, monuments to the sinfulness of the faithful. We all suffer through the sinfulness and limitation of the church's members, including its leaders.

This imperfection does not indicate that the church is not the extension of the life of Christ, but only that those who live the life of Christ in the church have not yet fully and finally made it their own. This is why sinners, even serious sinners, are not all automatically expelled from the church. They may have rejected the life of Christ through their sins, and to that extent are members of the church in an irregular and lifeless fashion. But they maintain a relationship with the church because the life of Christ once existed in them through grace and can be renewed if and when they repent.

Likewise, the church is not the kingdom of God, that final state that Jesus spoke of when all things are fully and finally enveloped in the love and glory of God. In the church, we have the beginnings of the kingdom. The church directs us toward the kingdom through its teaching and sanctifying activity as well as through our life together in the community. But the church here and now is not the kingdom, pure and simple.

For all that, the church is not optional, not something just for those who like organized religion while others are free to go it alone.

It is not possible to share the life of Christ and deliberately reject the church, because to reject the church is to reject the life of Christ.

This is not to say that all those who are not officially church members are automatically out of touch with the life of Christ. There are degrees of contact with the church and therefore degrees of membership in it. Not only baptized Catholics share the life of Christ, which is grace. Some Christians, for example, reverence God's Word in sacred Scripture and celebrate baptism, but not the other sacraments. Others accept almost the whole of the teaching of Christ and the church, but not the church's visible leadership (the pope and the bishops). Some people have never even heard of Christ, or never had Christ adequately presented to them, but strive to live their lives in reverence and responsibility. To all of these Christ offers a share in his life in some fashion.

Yet *full* incorporation in the church means living the life of grace, worshiping God with Christ in the liturgy and the sacraments, accepting church teaching and recognizing church authority. It is to this degree of full membership that Christ calls all humankind.

The life of the church, then, is the life of Christ, visible and active despite human faults and deficiencies. This community holds together in the holiness of Jesus' life, expressing and fostering that life in, through and for its members.

When Catholics reflect on the church, they reflect also on Mary, the mother of Jesus. This is not just because Mary had an essential role to play in the birth and life of Jesus, or because we revere her for her sinlessness, or because we rely on her intercession for us with Christ in heaven. All that is true, but there is more: Mary's part in the redemption and her continued association with Christ exemplify the church itself. Virgin and mother, Mary conceived Jesus through the intervention of the Holy Spirit and gave him to the world. So also, the church brings Christ into being in the faithful and offers him to the world not through its own human power, but through the power of the Holy Spirit. At the end of her life, Mary was assumed into heaven and now lives in glory with Christ—the state for which we believe the church is destined.

Mary has been called the model of the church. If we want to see the nature and the mission and the destiny of the church expressed and carried out in the life of just one of its members, we look to her. We turn to Mary to find out who and what we are as church.

For Discussion and Reflection
• *In what ways do you find Christ in the church?*
• *What have the sacraments meant in your life?*
• *How does the community of believers make a difference in your life?*

From the *Catechism of the Catholic Church*
Nos. 787–795; 1131–1134.

CHURCH

The Mission

The church shares Christ's life in space and time as the community of those living in grace. But the church is more than a spiritual club or a warm and friendly place to feel secure in our common participation in the life of Christ. When the Holy Spirit came upon the apostles at Pentecost, God gave the church a mission to address not just its own members but also the world at large, a mission in which all the church's members are called to collaborate.

The church's mission is to reshape creation into the image of Christ. Once God became human in Jesus, creation had a new goal, a new purpose: to reflect God as manifested in Jesus. The story of creation became the story of Christ. The love and reverence for God and humankind that was taught and exemplified in Jesus are to be manifested in every aspect of the world, in every human activity, in every human endeavor. This mission is carried out by church members—all of them—living and acting in the world, preparing for the final glorification of creation in the final coming of Christ.

The church is primarily an organization of laypeople. Priests and bishops are not the "real" believers, and other members of the church mere objects of their pastoral care. Neither does the value of a layperson's life depend merely on how much the person does in and for the church community. Laypeople—the primary members of the church—are baptized and confirmed believers whose main responsibilities lie outside church sanctuaries. The church exists to bring the life and love of Christ into the world, and the church's lay members live and work in the world. Therefore, laypeople bear prime responsibility for carrying out the church's mission in the world.

Consequently, one of the church's chief responsibilities is to enable laypeople to carry out their responsibilities *as laypeople* in the world. Church ministers, whether clerics or laypersons who work in the church, serve the general body of the church's members; they enliven and assist them in carrying out the church's mission of witness and action in the world.

Church members carry out this mission by acting in the person of Christ in their particular segment of the world. They are called to do as Christ did, namely to make holy, to teach, to lead. Church members make holy their segment of the world by manifesting the holiness of Christ and by inviting others to share that holiness. They teach by expressing in their lives the teaching of Christ and by living out its implications. In doing these things, church members lead the world toward its final destiny: complete life in Christ.

In practice, carrying out the church's mission is not a matter of pious posturing or preaching. Fulfilling the church's mission requires extending personal concern to those around us, changing situations offensive to human dignity, conscientiously and generously contributing to the destiny of creation, motivated not by greed or ambition, but by something—Someone—beyond the sphere of ordinary human activity. The believer in the world asks the question, "If Christ had his way here, how would things be?" The answer to that question provides the agenda for the believer's life and work, an agenda that often enough involves effort, sacrifice and misunderstanding. Carrying out the church's mission in the world is much more than just "being religious."

What is the scope of the church's mission? Every context in which the human person is involved calls for the presence of Christ and therefore for the witness and work of the Christian believer. Probably no complete list exists, but the basic human relationships are obviously included: family, friendships, marriage and the relationships we form in the course of our job or profession. Christ wishes to be present in all of these.

Also included are the more complex relationships that form the society in which we live: neighborhood, local and national government, unions, the courts. The way our country is run and, indeed, the way the world is run depend on human attitudes and human decisions and are therefore open to the influence of Christ working through those who believe in him.

Then there is culture, that complex of attitudes and practices that provide the day-to-day atmosphere in which we live. Our culture pays lip service to human worth and human dignity, but abuses humanity by abortion, pornography and racism, by tolerating poverty, by the canonization of wealth and power. Such a culture does not reflect the love and the life of Christ. The Christian believer has work to do here.

Human beings are active in still other contexts: sports and entertainment, the media, the academic world, science and medicine, industry. In fact, little goes on in the world that is not somehow affected by humankind, and all of it calls for life in Christ.

All of these human contexts need the influence of the life and love of Christ to be in final accord with God's love story for the world. They need to be remade in Christ's image—and that will happen not through some miraculous intervention from on high but through lay Christian believers conscientiously carrying out the mission of Christ's church in the world.

God wants to be in charge of the world through Christ. The world's destiny is the kingdom of God, full and acknowledged lordship exercised by Christ Jesus when he comes in glory at the end of time. The mission of the church is to work for the coming of that kingdom. This mission is exercised in every context in which a Christian believer lives out the implications of the life and teaching of Christ.

The reality of the church, both as community and in its mission to the world, is expressed most eloquently in the celebration of the Eucharist. At the celebration of Mass, the Christian community comes together under the leadership of its priest and in the company of Christ. We are instructed by God's Word in Scripture and the homily. We offer God the gift of our lives—all our actions, our thoughts, our words, our work, our relationships—symbolized by the bread and wine that is presented to the priest from the congregation.

Working through the priest, the Holy Spirit transforms these gifts into the Body and Blood of Christ. In the process, we relive with Christ the supreme moments of his earthly existence: his definitive offering of himself to the Father in his death on the cross. But now it is not his offering alone but ours as well.

When we receive Communion we receive the true and real Body and Blood of Christ, his soul and divinity, his risen life, to be the nourishment of our life in him. In the Eucharist, then, we are taught and sanctified. Our lives are given over again to Christ. We are strengthened in him.

But the Eucharist is not just a refuge, a chance to get away from our struggles and our problems in the world and spend some time together with Christ. The life of Christ in us is a life to be shared with the world around us. Every celebration of the Eucharist ends with an agenda for us. That agenda is God's will for the world, God's plan that the reality of Christ be brought into factory and store, neighborhood and office, friendship and family. It is an agenda whose conclusion will be expressed by Christ's coming again in glory to take all creation definitively to himself. We are not free to decline to work at the agenda because it is an integral part of the church's life, an integral part of our lives as believers, an integral part of the Eucharist.

The Eucharist is the heart of the church. It is an action of praise and love and thanksgiving to God on the part of the church, united with Christ. Its power impels us to bring to our world the energy and the life of Christ to prepare our world for final glorification in Christ. Everything the church is and does is somehow directed toward the Eucharist. Everything the church is and does somehow has its source in the Eucharist. We understand the church to the extent that we understand the Eucharist.

For Discussion and Reflection

- *Why is it important to think of the church as an organization primarily of laypeople?*
- *Name some concrete ways that church members whom you know carry out the church's mission in the world.*
- *In what ways do you carry out the mission of the church in your life?*

From the *Catechism of the Catholic Church*
Nos. 849–856; 897–900; 1324–1327.

CHAPTER TWELVE

TRINITY
The Source

As the story of creation, incarnation, redemption and church has unfolded in the context of human experience, another dynamic has been at work. A deeper theme gradually became clearer as Jesus' disciples reflected on their experience of Jesus' life, death and resurrection, as they set out to live, share and proclaim the life of Jesus in the church. This theme speaks not only of God's love for the human creature but also of the intimate, interior life of God before and beyond creation.

God has made us in the divine image, loved us in spite of our sinfulness, entered human history in Jesus, recreated us in the image of Jesus through the Holy Spirit and brought us together as church. In all those actions, God has also quietly and gently been telling us about what and who God is, about the power, sharing and love that were before the beginning, that are the source and form of everything, that are the goal to which everything is directed. Through our experience of creation and Jesus and church, God allows us to touch and to know the very divine center. God has revealed to us the mystery of the Trinity.

The triune God was part of the apostles' experience with Jesus and was at the center of their preaching. But, just as it took a long time for the church to learn to speak precisely about the full reality of Jesus, so only after several centuries of reflection was the church able to present a full, precise theological formulation about the Trinity. This formulation can be summarized in a few words. God is one; and in God are one divine nature and three divine Persons: Father, Son and Holy Spirit are in God. Son proceeds from Father, and Spirit from Father and Son.

What we are dealing with here is mystery. It is important to be clear about what we mean by *mystery* in a context like the Trinity. Mystery is not a problem to be solved, least of all a mathematical problem about how three can be one. Mystery is an inexhaustibly knowable truth, a reality beyond full comprehension, an expression of something which is understandable in part, but whose full significance is beyond human intelligence and human words.

What, then, does the experience of the apostles and the church enable us to understand about God?

Jesus spoke of God as Father, but in a way suggesting a deeper and more intense relationship than anyone had experienced or expressed before. God as Father meant something different to Jesus than it does to us. As the apostles (with the help of the Holy Spirit) reflected on their experience of Jesus, they came to understand that Jesus himself was nothing less than God. Jesus was not a copy of God, but himself God, fully human but also fully divine, fully known by God and fully knowing God.

Jesus promised to send the Holy Spirit upon the apostles. The Spirit came on Pentecost and enlivened them with a love and an energy never experienced before. The Spirit Jesus sent was not a ghost, not a metaphor, like "the spirit of Christmas past." The Spirit Jesus sent was nothing less than the love that is shared between Father and Son, a love of divine proportions, distinct from Father and Son, yet God as they are.

The church's experience of Jesus teaches us that in God is community, that God is source, that God is knowledge, that God is love. God is not some cold philosophical reality existing quietly and all alone; rather, God is one who knows and loves. God is Father, ultimate origin and power; God is Son, the Father's full self-knowledge, known and expressed so fully that the Son has a personhood of his own; God is Spirit, a love between Father and Son so intense that it expresses itself as distinct from Father and Son, yet one with them in being God. We speak of God as a Holy Trinity, a Holy "Threeness," three Persons yet one God.

As we reflect on what Jesus and the church have expressed in speaking of this innermost life of God, we associate creation with the Father, redemption with the Son, and the ongoing, loving life of Jesus in the church with the Holy Spirit. Yet we cannot deal appropriately with any of these episodes in the history of God's love for us unless we deal with them in the context of the Trinity, because the Trinity is the source and pattern of everything done and said in the story of God's relationship with creation, and all the Persons of the Trinity are involved in all aspects of creation, redemption and grace. The triune God is behind it all, a God who has wanted us to know who and what God is.

But two other matters are still unresolved. The first is this: Why didn't God just come out and tell us about the Trinity? Why were we left, as it were, to figure things out for ourselves based on what Jesus said and did and on what the young church experienced?

For the same reason that Jesus didn't just tell the apostles that he was God: the reality would have been so overwhelming as to be meaningless. The whole pattern of revelation before God became human had been intended to teach that God is one. Before anything else God had insisted that the Old Testament people learn that there are not many gods but one; that the realm of divinity is not a world of many competing powers but one unique, almighty Power; that the realm of divinity is not exhausted in the beauties and forces of creation but is something far beyond what we can see or imagine, much less portray in images.

Then, with Jesus, God made us ready for more. Through the power of Jesus' life, death and resurrection and through the enlightenment of the Holy Spirit we became capable of entering more deeply into knowledge of the personal life of God. God is still one, but it is the oneness of the Trinity. God didn't just tell us, because we learn best when we are shown rather than told. So God *showed* us about the Trinity through Jesus.

That still leaves the second unresolved matter: Why did God reveal the intimate life of the three divine persons to us? Why did Father, Son and Holy Spirit want us to know about their being, their relationship?

The answer is infinitely profound and yet infinitely simple: because God loves us.

When human beings love each other, they want to share themselves. They communicate. A mother will tell stories to her children about her youth, about how she met their father, about how things were in the early years of their marriage. She doesn't merely want to communicate information. She wants to communicate *herself* because she loves them and wants to share all she is with them.

Of course, complete communication between two human beings is impossible. None of us can really tell someone else everything about ourselves because we don't really know everything about ourselves. Yet in words and actions we continue to try because sharing ourselves is the center of loving, and the attempt to share continues as long as love lasts.

That's why God has shared the mystery of the Trinity with us: simply because God loves us. We can understand some of what God has shown us in revelation. Much, perhaps most, lies far beyond our powers of comprehension. In spite of that, God strives to share the truth of the inmost being of divinity with us because loving means sharing and God loves us.

But there is still more. God's communication with us is not limited to sharing information. God also intends us to share the very life and intimacy that has been shared by Father, Son and Holy Spirit since before the beginning of time. That's what we mean by glory.

For Discussion and Reflection

• *What would your faith life be like if you knew nothing about the Trinity?*

• *How does God's desire to tell us about himself compare to your experience of love?*

• *In your own prayer life, to which person of the Trinity do you most often turn? Why?*

From the *Catechism of the Catholic Church*
Nos. 234; 238–245.

CHAPTER THIRTEEN

GLORY

The Goal

The Father remakes us into the image of Christ through the action of the Holy Spirit so that we can live as Christ lives, not just here and now, in this mortal life, but in that future beyond time that we call eternity.

Jesus in heaven is both human and divine. He participates in the interior life of the Trinity that belonged to the Son before all ages. He also retains his humanity, now glorified after his death and resurrection. Because we share the full life of Christ, we, too, when our earthly life is over, will retain our humanity, glorified through our association with the Risen Christ, but somehow we will also share in his divinity. We will be who we are, but we will also be who he is, all that he is. Just as the Son became human to be like us, so, in the final scene of God's love story, we will have an eternal and glorious share in his being as God.

The words we use to describe the final goal that God has in store for us—words like *heaven, glory, eternal happiness*—are bland words, perhaps because we use them so casually. Their real meaning is difficult to imagine. We may conjure up images of angels and harps, but deep inside ourselves do we wonder whether a changeless eternity might not be just a bit boring? Therefore, let's examine more closely God's ultimate plan for us.

To begin, God's plan surpasses all understanding. It is mystery. God loves us so much that even he does not—perhaps cannot—fully express to us how things will be when we reach our goal.

Glory does not imply mere continuance of what we know and experience in our life now. We will somehow retain our individuality and our body, but we will be released from the constraints of the physical world, liberated from the body's capacity for suffering just as Christ is.

Glory also implies fulfillment. The potential that God created for each of us will not be lost but will be actualized and brought to term in the glorious humanity of Christ. Our capacity for loving and being loved, for intellectual achievement, for appreciating God's works, for communication with others, all the things we might have been but never got the chance to be, all the things we started but never got the chance to finish—all will be brought to completion in the life of Father, Son and Holy Spirit manifested in us and shared by us.

Likewise, the good that we have done and the blessings that we have received will still be ours. Recollect the finest moments we have experienced so far in our life: the love of family and friends spoken and shared, the few really generous and disinterested actions we have performed, the sense of accomplishment when we have finished a long and difficult project, the exhilaration we sometimes experience through music or poetry, the sense of awe and gratitude that occasionally comes in prayer or through liturgical celebration, all those wonderful moments of special intensity that we wish could last forever. All that will be ours in eternity, affirmed and enhanced beyond our wildest imagination in a glowing instant that will never end, validated by the love of Christ, transformed in the life of the Trinity.

Eternal glory, then, is a matter of intensity, of fullness of life. We do ourselves a disservice if we choose to think of it in terms of an endless succession or repetition of what we experience here and now.

Yet, the glory of heaven is not just something "out there." It has already begun "in here." Our life now provides, as it were, the basic material from which our eternal happiness will be formed. We don't sit back and wait for heaven while passing the time in meaningless human activity. We prepare ourselves for the glory of heaven by our thoughts, words and actions now. Heaven already has its roots in us.

Eternal glory is the flowering of the life of Christ that God has already planted in us and called on us to cultivate.

This explains the Christian view of death. Christian believers look on death not as an end, but as a change, as one moment in a continuity. Death is simply the final, definitive bottom line of our earthly life. At that instant, what we are is transformed to glory to the extent that what we have become in our lives is capable of being associated with Father, Son and Spirit in their life forever. Because nothing impure or tainted can be taken into the life of God, the marginal defects remaining when our earthly life ends are somehow purged and corrected by the action of God. That which is not capable of life in God—our sins, our selfishness, our rejections of God's love in the course of our human existence—is rejected.

We speak of this as the final judgment—but we do not mean judgment as a legal process in which God weighs evidence and then announces a sentence. Rather, this judgment is the final manifestation of what we really are when all pretense has been stripped away and all our hiding places closed to us, when we ourselves come to know our real goodness cleansed of earthly ambiguity.

If heaven's eternal glory is the full flowering of God's action in our lives and of our response to God's action, and if judgment is the manifestation of our relationship with God at death, then hell is simply the state of those who have no relationship with God to be transformed into glory. Hell is not a *place* in which God puts people who have not found favor. Hell is the *situation* of those who have deliberately closed themselves to participating in heaven by rejecting God's love. To be in hell is to have made oneself an eternal outsider. We don't like to think about hell, and the Christian life is certainly much more than striving to stay out of hell. But, if God has given us the freedom to accept and collaborate with the gifts we have been given, then God has also given us the possibility to reject those gifts entirely. God didn't create hell to keep us in line. Hell is merely the flip side of human liberty.

Each human life, then, is a process of getting ready for glory, of getting accustomed to being with and in Christ so that we are capable of enjoying his presence forever. It is the process of developing God's gifts in our life in such a way that they will fit into the life of the Trinity when our earthly life is over.

Heaven's glory, however, is more than relationships between God and individuals. It is a corporate affair. Heaven is an eternal sharing in the life of Christ, and, as we have already seen, sharing in the life of Christ is not something we do alone but as part of the community of all who share his life. In the state of glory we will not only be happy in the company of those we have personally known and loved during our lifetime, but we will also rejoice in the companionship of all those who have shared the life of Christ, consciously or unconsciously, from the beginning of the world to its final instant. The glory of each will be the glory of all. Heaven will be the ultimate church, the church first modeled by Mary the Mother of God, the community of all those who have accepted Christ, definitively transformed into the community of the blessed.

The glory of heaven is the goal for which God did everything that has been done in the story of the world, in the story of salvation. The world was created, humankind came to be and to act in the world, God became a human being who lived and died and rose from the dead, salvation was offered to sinners in and through Christ's church— all for the sake of God's glory, for the sake of our glory. From before the beginning God wanted us somehow to be part of the total happiness of Father, Son and Spirit. Into that happiness God has already begun to gather those whose earthly lives have come to an end. When the world's history will have reached its fulfillment, all who have answered God's call will live together in his glory.

The Trinity of Father, Son and Spirit is at the beginning of all that is, of all that happens. The Trinity of Father, Son and Spirit also stands at the end of it all, calling all of us to share in the glory of God.

For Discussion and Reflection

• *What role does the prospect of God's judgment play in your life?*
• *What things in your life give you hints about what heaven must be like?*
• *Do you look forward to sharing in God's glory?*

From the *Catechism of the Catholic Church*

Nos. 1023–1036.

CONCLUSION

Praying the Story

The story that began with creation, that unfolded through the history of human sinfulness and in the salvation brought to the world in the God-Man Christ, the story that continues through the teaching and mission of the church is about the glory of God. The glory of God, Father, Son and Spirit is the source in which the story has its origin and is the goal toward which the story is directed. That glory is our destiny because we are called to be part of Christ's story.

Our response to the call that is inherent in the story is, first of all, faith: believing what God tells us, accepting and responding to the love that God offers us in Christ. The response also includes expressing our faith in appropriate moral behavior, living in a way that is consistent with our calling to extend the life of Christ. In addition, the response involves certain religious practices that give external expression to our faith and deepen our life in Christ.

Pivotal to our life of faith is prayer, consciously lifting our minds and hearts to God in personal and corporate acknowledgment of God's goodness and generosity, of our own sinfulness and need. Prayer keeps us aware of who and what God is, of who and what we are, of where we have come from and where we are going. We might say that prayer is the self-consciousness of faith. There can be no real life of Christian faith without it.

The central prayer of the Christian life of faith is the Eucharist. In the eucharistic celebration the community of faith comes together to unite itself to the sacrifice of Jesus, to be nourished and strengthened by his risen life, to be energized for our responsibilities in God's world. In the Eucharist, Christian believers engage in remembrance and offering, remembrance of the story and offering of themselves.

It's important for us to *remember* the story, because, if we allow ourselves to forget it, our life will lose its whole purpose and meaning, or, at very least, will collapse into superficiality. Instead of moving forward to glory, we will spend our lives going around in circles, never really getting anywhere.

It's important for us, too, to *offer ourselves*, over and over again, to be part of the story. Otherwise the story becomes mere narrative of things past instead of a call to present faith and salvation.

The central prayer of the church is a prayer of remembrance and offering because remembrance and offering are central to faith.

The fourth of the regular Eucharistic Prayers that the church uses at Mass gives us the most extended and eloquent form of the story to pray. "Father . . . all your actions show your wisdom and love. You formed man in your own likeness and set him over the whole world to serve you, his creator, and to rule over all creatures. Even when he disobeyed you and lost your friendship, you did not abandon him to the power of death. . . . You so loved the world that in the fullness of time you sent your only Son to be our Savior . . . a man like us in all things but sin. . . . In fulfillment of your will he gave himself up to death; but by rising from the dead he destroyed death and restored life. . . . He sent the Holy Spirit from you, Father . . . to complete his work on earth and bring us the fullness of grace. . . . We now celebrate this memorial of our redemption. . . . We recall Christ's death . . . and, looking forward to his coming in glory, we offer you his body and blood, the acceptable sacrifice which brings salvation to the whole world."

In different ways, each of the other Eucharistic Prayers also speaks of remembrance and offering, because remembrance and offering are the heart of the eucharistic celebration and constitute its very meaning, just as remembrance and offering are the heart and meaning of our lives as believers.

While each Eucharistic Prayer has a little different form of remembering the story, the ending of each is the same. It's about Christ: "Through Him, with Him, in Him, in the unity of the Holy Spirit, all glory and honor is yours, almighty Father, for ever and ever." This is really a final summary of the story. The story is about Father, Son and Holy Spirit; it is about the glory of God. It's a glory that will never end. It's a glory in which we are called to share because we are called to share the life of God in Christ. It's a glory that we accept by remembering the story and by offering ourselves to Christ in faith.

That's what believing Catholic is all about.

For Discussion and Reflection

• *What do you remember and offer at Mass?*
• *Which of the four Eucharistic Prayers used at Mass is your favorite?*
• *Does it make sense for the church to expect its members to go to Mass on Sunday?*
• *Is it possible for a believing Catholic to be a pessimist?*

From the *Catechism of the Catholic Church*
Nos. 1359–1370; 1402–1405.

PART TWO

PRACTICING CATHOLIC

INTRODUCTION

Being Catholic involves faith, receiving God's gift of himself to us, accepting what God has told us about himself and ourselves through Scripture and the church, and responding accordingly. Being Catholic also involves commitment to certain standards of moral conduct. These are all essential components of professing Catholicism.

Yet being Catholic also involves certain specific religious behaviors, certain religious practices that arise from Catholic faith and tradition and which, taken together, constitute a way of being religious in a truly Catholic fashion, a way of being members of the church who are deliberately and consciously in touch with God in the context of the church. Part Two of this book is about those Catholic religious practices.

It has been said that Catholicism is as much a culture as a religion. In this sense "culture" means an integrated pattern of knowledge, belief and behavior that depends on experience and knowledge transmitted from one generation to another. It expresses the customary beliefs and social forms of a religious or social group. We all belong to one or more cultures: national, economic, ethnic; cultures determined by age and cultures determined by geography. The Catholic culture is that pattern of belief and behavior that gives us our identity as Catholic women and men, and "practicing" our Catholic faith means expressing who and what we are as members of the "Catholic culture," and, even more importantly, as members of the Catholic church.

To be a *practicing* Catholic, then, means more than just being a member of the church. Most fundamentally, it means giving external expression to our faith. Married people know that they have to express their love for one another. Otherwise, it will be taken for granted and ultimately grow cold. In exactly the same way, faith grows cold without religious expression. But this external expression of our faith has to be ongoing and regular. It has to be a practice. We have to practice our faith because what we do not practice we tend to lose. Anybody who has ever taken music lessons knows that. Practicing Catholics, therefore, are members of the church who consciously express their faith in ongoing and regular ways. They practice it.

It is significant to me that, when people say they have "been away" from the church for a while, they generally don't mean that they have stopped believing, or that they have stopped being members. They mean that they have stopped practicing. "Coming back to the church" means beginning to practice again.

There is always the danger of superficiality in religious practice. It is possible for people to go through religious motions without having faith at all. But I am inclined to think that going through the motions of Catholic practice is better than doing nothing at all about our faith. Religious practice can hold things together for us during periods when our interior dispositions are in turmoil. Religious practice is not only an expression of what we are, but also a reminder to us of what we are supposed to be.

There is still another dimension to being a practicing Catholic. Catholic practice is indeed an expression and support of our interior faith, a constant exercise in being what God has called us to be. But Catholic practice is also a sign to others of our religious commitment. Obviously, we do not practice our faith in order to impress other people. But our Catholic practice does say something to other people: something about us, something about the church and something about the Lord. It gives some indication to ourselves to what degree *we* really belong to the church (and to the Lord), and it lets others see what *really* belonging means.

In the chapters that follow, I will deal with Catholic religious practice, with the fundamental religious activities that express our faith and our membership in the church, that strengthen them and that proclaim them to others. There is, as I have said, more to being a Catholic than the religious practices that I will deal with, and there are more practices that Catholics observe than I will write about. But it is my hope that what I have to say will help people become more conscious of what their Catholic faith involves in practice and how the practice serves to strengthen and express that faith.

CHAPTER ONE

GOING TO MASS ON SUNDAY (AND HOLY DAYS)

If it were a felony to be a practicing Catholic, what kind of evidence would be sufficient to convict somebody? Probably regular attendance at Sunday Mass. Regular attendance at Sunday Mass is the basic Catholic practice. Once you have stopped going to Mass on Sunday, although you are still a member of the church you really aren't a practicing Catholic any more.

The *Catechism of the Catholic Church* (#2181) says that "the Sunday Eucharist is the foundation and confirmation of all Christian practice." It is the foundation and confirmation of all Christian practice because of what happens at the Sunday Eucharist. When we go to Mass on Sunday, we gather with the Christian community in order to hear the Word of God and take part again in the passion and resurrection of the Lord Jesus. Listening to the Word of God and sharing the life, death and resurrection of Christ in the community of believers are the basic elements of our faith and thus are also the basic constituents of Christian practice.

We need to hear the Word of God because the Word of God gives direction and sense to our human existence. God's Word tells us who we are, what we have been given and what is expected of us. But participation in the Sunday Eucharist is more than a learning session. It is also a renewal of our sharing in the life, death and resurrection of Jesus, a sharing that constitutes the very essence of our being as Christian believers. Being a Christian believer means living the life of Christ, the Christ who spent his years on earth giving himself for other human beings, who died because of his faithfulness to his heavenly Father, who rose to a new kind of life that was extended to everyone who would believe in him and that would last forever. When we participate in the celebration of the Eucharist, we return to our roots as believers and are strengthened in the dimensions of our existence that give us energy and meaning. We need this renewal, and we need it regularly because it is so easy to let the life of Christ in us grow thin and meaningless. Without regular contact with the Risen Christ, we run the risk of forgetting who he is and who we are.

We also need contact with the community. We need to be reassured that we do not live the life of Christ in solitude but are part of a larger body in which Christ lives and teaches and sanctifies.

Moreover, our participation in the Sunday Eucharist is not just for us. It is also a testimony to others—believers and nonbelievers—of our faithfulness to Christ, of our communion in faith and love. When we go to Mass on Sunday, we are strengthened, and we strengthen others as well.

This is why the church makes it quite plain that we are obliged to attend Sunday Mass. It's a sin to miss, not just because missing constitutes a violation of church law, but also because missing is damaging to my faith and harmful to the faith of others. My life isn't complete without regular contact with the Risen Christ, and the Christian assembly isn't complete without my presence. "Obligation" isn't a popular word, but we are obliged to participate in Sunday Mass simply as a consequence of being Catholic Christian believers. It's part of what we have signed on for. Neglecting Sunday Mass is simply inconsistent with what we profess to be.

In this context, it is appropriate to say something about the complaint of those who say they "don't get anything out of it." Sunday Mass is indeed supposed to give us something—God's Word, renewal of our life in faith, contact with the Risen Christ and with Christian community. But Sunday Mass is also a call to give, to give ourselves once more to the Risen Christ in faith, to dedicate ourselves to the service of our neighbor, to offer our lives to the community of believers. If we only expect to get something, we are overlooking a major aspect of what the Sunday Eucharist is about.

This is why we are called to "participate" in the Eucharist, to put ourselves into what is happening and make our contribution to the action of the community. We are invited to sing, to respond to the prayers, to engage ourselves with the other participants, to engage ourselves with the Lord. The Sunday Eucharist is not something we attend, as if it were a performance that we may or may not find satisfying. It is something in which we have a part to play: it is something that we do. If we find that we "don't get anything out of it," the reason may be that we are insufficiently conscious of what we are supposed to put into it. And that which we are supposed to put into it is nothing less than ourselves reaching out to Christ with the rest of the community, receiving his word and his love in the company of the church. Just being there isn't really enough.

An important dimension of the Sunday Eucharist is its variety. Of course, certain aspects of it are always the same. There are always readings from Scripture. There is always the formal Eucharistic Prayer. There is always Holy Communion. But the tonality of the Sunday Eucharist varies throughout the church's year.

In Advent, we concentrate on the coming of Christ, his final coming at the end of time and his first coming as a child in Bethlehem. During the Christmas season, we recall the events of the early life of Jesus. Lent is a season of repentance and renewal in preparation for reliving the death and resurrection of Christ during Holy Week and Easter. The Easter season recalls how Christ manifested himself after his Resurrection and how the church started up and grew. The most extensive part of the church year is what is called "Ordinary Time," stretching from the end of the Christmas season to the beginning of Lent and from the end of the Easter season to the beginning of Advent. These weeks symbolize the ongoing life of God's people, extending the life of Christ and headed toward his coming at the end of time.

The purpose of these variations is not to keep the congregation from getting bored, but to put the people in touch with all the aspects of the life of Christ and to allow Christ's life to color their own existence with the meaning of his existence. The church's year invites us to apply the life of Christ to our life and to offer our life to him as it changes and develops.

"Holy days of obligation" are special feasts in the church's year on which Catholics are also expected to participate in the Eucharist just as they are on Sunday. These feasts celebrate important aspects of our faith that, for various reasons, do not fall into the regular Sunday pattern. In the United States these feasts are Christmas (December 25), the feast of Mary the Mother of God (January 1), the Assumption of Mary (August 15), All Saints Day (November 1) and the feast of the Immaculate Conception (December 8). (Some years ago, for practical reasons, the bishops of the United States determined that the Mass obligation would not apply to these feasts, except for Christmas and the Immaculate Conception, when they fall on Saturday or Monday.)

The word *eucharist* means "thanksgiving" and, in the final analysis, participating in the eucharistic celebration on Sundays and feast days is about thanksgiving. When we go to Mass, we listen to the Word of God with thanksgiving. We gratefully participate in the death and resurrection of Christ and receive the Lord in Holy Communion. We offer the Lord our joys and our sorrows, our problems and our achievements in gratitude for his share in them, and we leave the assembly thankful to take the Lord with us out into our everyday world.

Being a practicing Catholic means being gratefully in touch with the Lord. Our life as believers is supposed to be an ongoing act of thanksgiving, and that sense of gratitude is expressed and sharpened and nourished and energized to a unique degree when we come together each Sunday for Mass. That's why being a practicing

Catholic necessarily involves participation in the Sunday eucharistic celebration.

For Discussion and Reflection

• *Why do you go to Mass on Sunday?*
• *To what extent do you "participate" in the Sunday Eucharist?*
• *How does the church's liturgical year affect your life?*

From the *Catechism of the Catholic Church*
Nos. 2177–2178; 2180–2182.

CHAPTER TWO

RECEIVING THE SACRAMENTS

Next to going to Mass on Sunday, the most characteristic Catholic practice is what we speak of as "receiving the sacraments." This phrase is part of our basic Catholic vocabulary, but it's not completely exact.

For one thing, when people speak of the practice of receiving the sacraments, they generally aren't referring to all the sacraments (including matrimony, anointing of the sick and confirmation). They are referring to Holy Communion and confession. These are the "regular" sacraments that Catholics know they are supposed to receive with some frequency as a matter of habit and practice. The others are what we might call "special event" sacraments.

Second, speaking about "receiving" the sacraments doesn't do full justice to what happens at Holy Communion and confession. There is a sense in which we "receive" in these sacraments. We receive the body and blood of Christ in Holy Communion, and we receive absolution in confession. Moreover, these sacraments (like all the rest of the sacraments) are gifts from God that we cannot earn or deserve. We can only receive. But there is also a dimension of "doing" in the sacraments. We are not merely passive recipients but collaborative agents in the sacramental action.

With that in mind, we can now say something about Holy Communion and confession, about what's involved in "receiving the sacraments."

Most Catholics treasure going to Communion. They gratefully remember their First Communion as an important step in growing up Catholic or becoming Catholic. They know that receiving Communion is supposed to be an ordinary part of attending Mass. They understand that, when they receive Communion, they receive Christ, "body and blood, soul and divinity," not just as a temporary visitor, but also as a source of energy and direction for their lives. They know that Holy Communion is one of the most basic ways in which they stay in touch with the Lord and strengthen his life in them.

As a bare minimum, the church expects Catholics to receive Communion at least once a year during the Easter season. If you don't receive the Lord at least then, you aren't really practicing your faith.

But receiving Communion is not something to be done thoughtlessly. The church expects us to give some reflection and preparation to receiving the Lord. As an encouragement to preparation and to symbolize our hunger for the Lord, the church requires that we not eat or drink (except for water and medicine) for an hour before Communion.

More importantly, if we have turned away from the Lord through serious sin, we are not in a fit state to receive him in the Eucharist. There's no point in trying to strengthen Christ's life in us if we have rejected that life through our own sinfulness. We first have to return to the Lord through the sacrament of reconciliation. This is why Catholics who have entered an invalid marriage and who continue to live together as husband and wife may not receive Communion. Objectively speaking, they are in a state of sinfulness, and that state has to be corrected before receiving Communion will do them any good.

But even more is required of us than the eucharistic fast and being in the state of grace. As I said earlier, we have a part to play in the sacrament. Our part is to give ourselves consciously and generously to the Lord who gives himself to us. Holy Communion is a profession of faith on our part, a renewal of our commitment to Christ and his church. Unless we are careful about doing our part in the Eucharist, receiving Communion can easily become a mere formality.

Sometimes Catholics wonder why those who are not Catholic are not supposed to receive Communion when they attend Mass. It's not a matter of denying people something or of being inhospitable, but a matter of consistency. Those who do not share the full Catholic faith should not engage in the profession of full Catholic faith that is implicit in receiving Communion. They cannot conscientiously say "Amen" to all that the reception of the Eucharist involves.

Now let's talk about confession. The sacrament of reconciliation is one of the more complex sacraments. Even the name by which we call it is manifold. The *Catechism of the Catholic Church* (#1423 and following) gives four names to this sacrament in addition to "confession": the sacrament of conversion, the sacrament of penance, the sacrament of forgiveness and the sacrament of reconciliation. These names link the sacrament to Jesus' call to conversion and penance, to his offer of forgiveness and reconciliation with his heavenly Father.

In this sacrament, the sinner comes to the priest to acknowledge his or her offenses. Presenting oneself for the sacrament is itself an act of faith and an act of confidence in the mercy of God. There would be no point in coming if we didn't believe that God welcomed us there. We tell the priest our sins and express our sorrow, and, in the name of God and the church, the priest pronounces us absolved of our sins and assigns us a symbolic act of reparation for our sins.

Sometimes people wonder why they can't just tell God they are sorry for their sins and have God forgive them "directly." There are two reasons. The first is that we need to engage a representative of God in honestly facing our sins and to hear personally and immediately from that representative that God has forgiven us. The potential for self-deception is too great to settle for anything else. The second reason is that our sins have not just offended God. They have also weakened the holiness of the church at large and thus offended all the church's members. Therefore, we not only have to seek forgiveness and reconciliation from God, but from the church as well. When the priest gives us absolution for our sins, he speaks both in the name of God and in the name of God's people, which is the church.

This communal dimension of the sacrament of reconciliation has become clearer through the communal penance services that parishes offer during Advent and Lent. We gather with other members of the church. We hear God's offer of forgiveness proclaimed in the words of sacred Scripture. We confess our sins and receive absolution individually, but all around us are other people who are doing the same thing. Thus, the church teaches us that sin is not something just between us and God, but also something that involves the whole community of believers.

How often should we "go to confession"? The church's law tells us that, if we have serious sins, sins that have separated us from the life of Christ, we are expected to participate in the sacrament at least once a year. To remain deliberately in a state of detachment from the life of Christ and the church for more than that signifies that we are not really serious about our participation in God's people. We aren't really practicing our faith.

But that's a minimum. Those who are in serious sin should seek forgiveness of God and the church as soon as possible. Even those who are not conscious of serious sin need the sacrament because it serves to call us to attentiveness to our lack of generosity, to our selfishness, to our lack of concern for our responsibilities to others. Little sins can grow into big sins if we don't deal with them promptly. We probably should deal with our sins in the sacrament of reconciliation at least as often as we pay our bills or get our car serviced.

Often Catholics seem to give the impression that they don't look forward to going to confession in the same way they look forward to going to Communion. They look on Communion as a privilege and on confession as a duty, the duty of dealing with their guilt. But confession is not just about guilt. It is also about God's love and God's mercy, the same love and mercy that we celebrate in the sacrament of the Eucharist.

The sacrament of the Eucharist and the sacrament of reconciliation are about the basics of our Christian life: our need for God's love and presence and mercy, our sharing in the community of those who believe. That's why participating in them regularly is such a fundamental part of being a practicing Catholic.

For Discussion and Reflection
- *How do you express your self-gift to Christ in Holy Communion?*
- *Do you like to go to confession? Why? Why not?*
- *What part does community play in your reception of the Eucharist and the sacrament of reconciliation?*

From the *Catechism of the Catholic Church*
Nos. 1391–1398; 1440–1449.

CHAPTER THREE

PRAYING

Praying is a less public and organized Catholic practice than the ones we have considered so far, but it is still central to being a practicing Catholic.

In its most basic form, prayer is consciously spending time with God. The classic definition calls it raising our minds and hearts to God. "Saying prayers," using set forms of words to address ourselves to God, is only the surface of prayer. What counts is what goes on in our hearts.

That's not to say that words are unimportant. They give structure to our prayer. They remind us of how to pray and for what to pray. They serve as a sort of primer for our prayer, to point us in the right direction and get us started. Sometimes in prayer we just don't know what to talk about with God. The prayers that we have learned by heart remind us of what we are invited to bring before the Lord.

The greatest formal prayer of all is the Lord's Prayer, the prayer that Jesus taught his disciples when they asked him to teach them about prayer. Saint Thomas Aquinas says that the Our Father teaches us what things we ought to pray for as well as the order in which we should pray for them. Every Christian believer knows the Our Father by heart. We pray it together every time we gather to celebrate the Eucharist.

Another important prayer for practicing Catholics is the rosary. In the rosary, we pray the Our Father and the Hail Mary (the other basic Catholic prayer) over and over again as we reflect on the events in the life of Christ and his mother. As is the case with the Our Father itself (and with every other formula of prayer), the real kernel of the matter does not lie in saying the words, but in letting the words lift up our minds and hearts to make contact with the Lord and with the meaning of his life for us.

Then there are meal prayers, the blessing and thanksgiving we express when we sit down to eat. These prayers serve to remind us of our dependence on God and of the gratitude for his goodness to us that is one of the most basic factors in Catholic Christian spirituality.

Many of us were trained as children to say morning and night prayers, offering ourselves to God at the beginning of the day and presenting ourselves to God again at the end. Sometimes people "grow out" of morning and night prayers, and this is a pity, since all of us need regular daily contact with the Lord in order to preserve a dimension of meaning in our lives. For that matter, there is also the fact that all of us always remain children in the face of God. We never get so mature that we no longer need our Father.

One element in our night prayers ought to be the Act of Contrition, expressing our sorrow to God for the ways in which we have failed him throughout the day. The purpose of regular use of the formal Act of Contrition is not to keep us feeling guilty, but to keep us aware of who and what we are: poor sinners that God loves and stands ready to forgive.

The prayer formulas that we use are a kind of tool kit for practicing Catholics. There are tools for every occasion, and it's good for us to have them handy. But the important thing is not just having the tools. The important thing is knowing how to use them to be in touch with the Lord.

Other prayers are more spontaneous: "God help me," as the truck bears down on us; "Thank you, Jesus," as the rain clears on picnic day. We can be in touch with the Lord for no particular reason, just because we love him, as we wait for a traffic light to change or for someone to answer our telephone call. Prayer means being attentive to the Lord whenever and however we can, attentive to the Lord who is always attentive to us.

Praying together is important, too. Jesus told his followers that, wherever two or three of them are gathered in his name, he is there in the midst of them (see Matthew 18:20). When a prayer group meets or a family says grace before meals, it's not just a matter of individuals relating to the Lord at the same time, but of a deeper and richer presence of the Lord in the context of their prayer together. We receive the Lord from one another and offer the Lord to one another when we pray in common.

Father Patrick Peyton spent most of his priestly ministry teaching people that "The family that prays together, stays together." This is because families that pray together weld themselves into a unity in the Lord that is even stronger than the natural bonds of family affection. One might say that healthy Christian families always require one more member, and that member is the Lord Jesus consciously sought and acknowledged in prayer.

An especially important form of family prayer for the church is the Liturgy of the Hours, a traditional collection of psalms and readings that priests and religious are expected to pray as part of their vocation but that is increasingly being used by laypersons as well. Some parishes regularly schedule morning and evening prayer from the Liturgy of the Hours. This way of praying has been designated as the official prayer of the church in which the individuals who pray unite themselves with the church universal in their attentiveness to the Lord. It is the family prayer of the church.

Sometimes when people tell us of their crosses and their needs, we tell them that we will say a prayer for them. What does that mean? It doesn't mean that we will inform God of their situation so that God will pay attention to them. It means that we will stand with them before God in their time of trial, that we want to share their suffering, that we offer ourselves as God's instruments to care for them, that we acknowledge that their need is our need because we are all one in the Body of Christ.

It's the same when we ask other people to pray for us. When we do that, we are saying that we know that we can't make it on our own, that we are vulnerable, that we need the attentiveness of God and that that attentiveness generally comes to us from the Lord through one another.

Praying for other people and being prayed for by others are ways in which we acknowledge our interdependence in God's love for us. We are never alone. We are never alone even with God. We are always together in the Lord. That's one of the most important lessons of prayer.

Prayer is not some form of magic, the recitation of a set formula of words that yields specific guaranteed results. Prayer is not just an obligation that we are expected to fulfill. Prayer is keeping ourselves in touch with the Lord and inviting the Lord to be in touch with us, whether as a parish gathered officially in church on Sunday, whether as a family saying grace, whether as a group of priests praying vespers together before dinner, whether as a seemingly solitary individual quietly praying the Angelus at noon in an office or on the work site. Because the presence of the Lord is what gives meaning to our lives, prayer is the life's breath of the Christian believer.

To pray only occasionally is to make a weak and thin life for ourselves. To pray regularly, at specific times and in specific ways day by day, is to allow the Lord to play a major role in our human existence. To pray "always"—in every circumstance and at every opportunity— as Jesus commanded his disciples (see Luke 18:1) and as Saint Paul recommended to the early Christians (see Romans 12:12; Colossians 4:2; 1 Thessalonians 5:17) is to invite and allow the Lord to be part of everything we do. Being a practicing Catholic means being a practitioner of prayer.

For Discussion and Reflection

• *What are your favorite forms of prayer? Why?*
• *How is prayer part of your life?*
• *What does the Our Father teach us?*

From the *Catechism of the Catholic Church*

Nos. 2559–2565; 2634–2636.

CHAPTER FOUR

VISITING THE BLESSED SACRAMENT

The Lord is present in our lives in many different ways. He is with us when we are at Mass on Sunday. He comes to us when we receive him in Holy Communion and when we celebrate his forgiveness in the sacrament of reconciliation. The Lord is with us when we pray. The Lord is also present for us in the consecrated eucharistic Bread that we reserve in the tabernacle in our churches.

Originally, there were no tabernacles because there were no Christian churches—buildings dedicated exclusively to the worship of God. When the Christian faith was given social and legal standing, churches as we know them began to be built. At some point, Holy Communion began to be reserved in the churches for the sick who might need it in preparation for their death. The reserved Sacrament was reverently kept in a special but not conspicuous place.

As the centuries passed, the church developed new ways of responding to the goodness and presence of the Lord. Among these was the practice of offering adoration to the reserved Sacrament, to the Lord present—Body and Blood, Soul and Divinity—under the sacred species. As this practice grew, it seemed more fitting to keep the Blessed Sacrament in a more prominent place. Ornate chests and wall closets were used until, in the late sixteenth century, it became common to keep the Blessed Sacrament permanently in a tabernacle, an ornate locked container in the middle of the main altar of the church.

About the same time, the liturgy of the Mass was growing more and more distant from those who attended. They no longer understood its language. Singing was reserved for the choir. The only thing that seemed to matter was that the Lord was somehow there. So, in the minds of many, the real presence of the Lord in the Eucharist became more important than the celebration of the death and resurrection of Jesus in the Mass.

People liked to look at the consecrated host. Priests were expected to prolong the elevation of the host after the consecration so that everybody had a chance to see it. In time, it became customary to put the eucharistic Bread into a special container, called a monstrance, so that people could look at it and pray to it for hours or even days at a time. Seeing the host, at benediction or during the annual Forty Hours' Devotion, became the high point of eucharistic devotion for generations of Christian believers.

The Second Vatican Council called for a refocusing of perspective. The center of Christian life was to be the celebration of the eucharistic sacrifice of the Mass, in which people heard the word of God proclaimed, in which they united themselves once more with the sacrifice of Christ, in which they received the Lord in Holy Communion. Attention to the presence of Christ in the reserved Sacrament was not discouraged, but was to be seen in relationship with the Mass in which Christ is with us as food, medicine and comfort, a presence to be assimilated more than contemplated. The adoration of the Blessed Sacrament was to be in harmony with the liturgy, to take its origin from the liturgy and to orient people to the liturgy.

Adoration of the Blessed Sacrament, contact with the real presence of Christ, even outside Mass, still has an important place in Catholic practice. It is an expression of the desire of individual Christians to spend time with the Lord Jesus, to cultivate a deeper personal intimacy with him, to make contact with the humanity of the Lord God in his nearness to us, just to be together with him as we are together with our friends. Almost spontaneously, when Catholics enter a church, even if they are there to see the art works, they will first find the tabernacle, genuflect and spend a moment or two in a quiet visit with the Lord. This is as it should be.

Catholics are glad that the Lord is near them. They like to think of him as having an address in their neighborhood, a place where he can always be found to listen to them and to spend time with them. Visiting the Blessed Sacrament, at least occasionally, is part of being a practicing Catholic. It is an acknowledgment of the accessibility of the Lord. He's not far off somewhere. His eucharistic presence is no more distant than the nearest church building.

Some parishes organize perpetual adoration of the Blessed Sacrament. They arrange to have parishioners in the presence of their eucharistic Lord around the clock, twenty-four hours a day, seven days a week. There is never a moment in these communities in which some member is not praying for the needs of the parish and the diocese, for vocations, for social justice, for the conversion of sinners. This is a praiseworthy practice because it highlights not only our ongoing need for the Lord's intervention in our lives but also the continuous desire of the Lord to be in touch with his people. Parishes that have perpetual adoration find a special vigor in their parish life.

Sometimes questions arise in connection with devotion to the real presence of Jesus in the Blessed Sacrament. Often parishioners will request their pastor to provide perpetual exposition of the Blessed Sacrament, having the Sacred Host always visible in the monstrance. They are puzzled when this is not thought to be appropriate. The church does not encourage perpetual exposition for several reasons. One is that exposition of the Blessed Sacrament is supposed to be a special event, a time of particular intensity when people gather in greater numbers to offer special adoration to the Lord. To make this an ordinary thing is to deprive it of its specialness. It would be like trying to have Christmas every day. Another reason why the church does not encourage perpetual exposition of the Blessed Sacrament is that it tends to preempt the other activities that take place in the parish church. When the Blessed Sacrament is solemnly exposed in the monstrance, it is supposed to be the center of attention. Nothing else should take people's attention away from it. This is hard to reconcile with the ongoing activities of a parish church, such as Masses and weddings and funerals.

Another question that arises in connection with devotion to the real presence is the positioning of the tabernacle in our churches. Many of us grew up accustomed to having the tabernacle on the main altar, the center of the congregation's attention. This was not inappropriate when the priest celebrated the Eucharist with his back to the people, facing the tabernacle. But when it became customary for the celebrant to face the people so as to symbolize his contact with them as a representative of Christ, he would often find himself with his back to the reserved Sacrament. Moreover, having the tabernacle on or behind the altar made for two different centers of attention when Mass was being celebrated. For these reasons, it is now customary, when churches are built or renovated, to provide another place for the tabernacle, away from the main altar. The purpose is not to downplay the importance of the real presence in the church, but to make clear that the presence of Christ in our midst is manifold. One is the dynamic presence of Christ in the celebration of the Eucharist with his people, symbolized by the freestanding altar of sacrifice. Another is the ongoing presence of Christ in the reserved Sacrament, symbolized by placing the tabernacle apart from the altar where it can receive special attention. It is the same Christ, of course, but it is important to keep clear that the celebration of Mass and the reservation of the Eucharist are different aspects of the Lord's care for us.

In Evelyn Waugh's novel *Brideshead Revisited* (which many consider one of the great Catholic novels of our century), there is a scene in which Lord Brideshead tells his sister and brother that the bishop wants to close the chapel in their family castle. The teenaged sister, Cordelia, says, "We must have the Blessed Sacrament here. I like popping in at odd times." Our Lord offers himself to us as a neighbor whom we can stop in to see whenever we feel inclined, and popping in on the Lord is part of being a practicing Catholic.

For Discussion and Reflection

• *How would your life be different if there were no Blessed Sacrament reserved in your church?*

• *How does the Vatican II emphasis on the centrality of the Mass influence your devotion to the Blessed Sacrament?*

• *How often do you "pop in" on the Blessed Sacrament?*

From the *Catechism of the Catholic Church*
Nos. 1373–1378; 1418.

CHAPTER FIVE

DOING PENANCE AND EXERCISING SELF-CONTROL

The church's formal laws of penance are relatively simple. From the age of fourteen, Catholics are required to abstain from meat on Ash Wednesday and the Fridays of Lent (including Good Friday). From age eighteen to fifty-nine, they are also to fast (that is, eat only one full meal) on Ash Wednesday and Good Friday. Substantial observance of these laws is a matter of serious obligation. Catholics are also encouraged to observe abstinence on Fridays throughout the year and to observe the whole season of Lent as a time of special penance.

The church does not call us to acts of penance because we have to earn the mercy and forgiveness of God. God's pardon is not something that we can deserve through our own effort. It is a gift. The church calls us to acts of penance because it is important for us to remember that we are sinners, that we have misused God's gifts for our own selfish purposes, that we are in constant need of God's mercy. When we do without meat on Friday or eat less on fast days, we are reminding ourselves that we owe God. We do without something that we could otherwise rightfully have in order to recall what we have wrongfully taken and used for ourselves. Acts of penance are not a payback that evens the score, but a way of recalling that we are constantly in God's debt.

It is traditional for practicing Catholics to "do something for Lent" beyond the little bit that is required of us by church law. For many, doing without meat on the Fridays and fasting on Ash Wednesday and Good Friday are not really very significant, or are only a beginning.

The classical Catholic agenda for Lent is fasting, prayer and almsgiving. Fasting, in addition to the canonical fast, can consist in doing without some of our crutches for a while: the extra cup of coffee in the morning, the drink before dinner. Lenten prayer can consist in going to Mass each day or praying the rosary on the way to work. Almsgiving (a rather archaic word for most of us) means doing works of mercy. This might involve special monetary contributions to the St. Vincent de Paul Society or an extra visit to someone we know in a nursing home. The important thing is not the specific practices that we undertake, but the heightened awareness of our need for forgiveness that the practices symbolize and the willingness to open ourselves up to the action of the Lord that they express.

Lent is an important season for Catholics. It's a kind of spring training or wake-up call that the church gives us each year, an invitation to take stock of our lives and to allow God to put things back in order there. It's easy enough to overlook Lent or to do the bare legal minimum, but if we settle for that, we are missing a significant opportunity to join with the rest of the church in a renewal of our individual and corporate Christian identity.

There is another facet of the practice of our Catholic faith that calls for some consideration here, and that is the ordinary practice of Christian self-control or self-discipline. This is not so much a matter of actions that are meant to keep us conscious of our sinfulness, but rather of a way of living that keeps us growing and developing in the presence and action of God in our lives. If penance is aimed at dealing with the bad habits in our lives, Christian self-control is aimed at acquiring good ones.

We are all creatures of habit. Over a period of time, we do things in a certain place and in a certain way. We get up at a certain time in the morning. We change clothes when we come home from work. We grocery shop every week on the same day. Habits are ways that we have found to take care of the small change of our lives without having to start from scratch each time. Our habits become second nature to us, but in order for them to take hold we have to do them over and over again. Similarly, when we want to change habits, it takes extra effort and attention. Probably everybody has had the experience of turning down the usual street to go home for a week or two after we have moved somewhere else.

The practice of Christian life requires habits, too. We go to Mass on Sunday because that's our habit. We don't sit down and decide every Saturday what we are going to do tomorrow. We just do it because we have done it for a long time. It's now part of our life. We say morning and evening prayers and prayers before meals because we have always done so. These are our habitual prayers.

But at some point, the habit had to be formed. Consciously or unconsciously we decided over and over again (or our parents helped us decide) that these actions would be part of our regular existence. We took control of this aspect of our lives and disciplined ourselves to make it part of us. If there had not been some decision and some practice, there would be no habit.

Forming habits is not necessarily easy. Other opportunities present themselves on a Sunday morning or we are tired when it's time for night prayers. The practice that seemed so right before now appears inconvenient or irksome. But we do it anyway, and the habit becomes a little stronger in us because we have exercised a little disciplined self-control.

Sometimes, however, habits seem to come about spontaneously. Without really realizing it, we suddenly find that we are late for work every day or that we don't have time to pray anymore. This is because there is a kind of default setting within us that inclines us to that which is easy, effortless, immediately satisfying. We seem to be programmed to self-indulgence, and if we do not form other habits, the habits of self-indulgence will take over.

Basic Christian self-control or self-discipline is the way we keep control of our habits. We keep the good ones in force, we work at diminishing the bad ones and we strive to acquire appropriate new ones. This requires a certain degree of attentiveness on our part. Committed Christians have always found the practice of a daily examination of conscience important for their lives. The purpose is not so much to keep ourselves conscious of guilt, but to take regular stock of our life to see where some attention is required. Did I pray today? If not, why not? Did I watch what I said when I was talking about the fellow worker I find difficult? What can I do to make things better between us?

The fact of the matter is that we are forming habits all the time, good ones, indifferent ones or bad ones. We need to exercise regular control over our habits because, if we don't, we may suddenly find ourselves with a whole load of unacceptable ones that we now have to struggle to uproot. It would have made more sense to deal with them when they were new.

The word *discipline* means learning, and when we say that Christian life requires discipline, we are saying that we have to keep learning about ourselves. *Discipline* also means an orderly pattern of behavior, and exercising discipline in our lives means the constant effort to acquire a life pattern for ourselves that is in accord with who and what we are as Christian believers. It means deliberately putting our faith in control of our lives. We never reach the point where we can do without discipline or self-control simply because the Lord is always teaching us something more, because there are always new ways of responding to what God has called us to be.

Penance and self-control are not the same thing. One has to do with past sins, the other with present and future habits. But they have two things in common. One is that they are not always appealing. They can be demanding and difficult. The other is that they are both necessary to preserve a healthy realism in our life as practicing Catholics.

For Discussion and Reflection

• *What penitential practices have you undertaken during Lent? How were they connected with your life?*

• *What are your good habits and bad habits? How did you get them?*

• *How is Christian self-control a challenge?*

From the *Catechism of the Catholic Church*

Nos. 1430–1439; 2012–2016.

CHAPTER SIX

GETTING MARRIED IN THE CHURCH

When we talk about "getting married in the church," it's important to distinguish between the marriage and the wedding. The wedding can involve all sorts of things like rented tuxes and limos and the selection of the music, photographers and the hall for the reception. Sometimes people go overboard on things like this, but that's understandable because a wedding is an important event.

Marriage, on the other hand, is the reason we have a wedding. Marriage is the lifetime contract or covenant by which the bride and groom give themselves to each other in faith before God for the rest of their lives. "Getting married in the church" means making this contract in the context of the community of faith. To get married in the church it's not essential, or even necessary to have a big (and expensive) wedding. What is essential for a Catholic marriage is that the bride and groom express the appropriate commitment to each other in the presence of representatives of the church (generally a priest and two witnesses). The reason this is essential is that every marriage is a church event.

Marriage is a church event for a number of reasons. For one thing, it's a sacrament. When baptized persons "get married in the church," the action of Christ is involved. Christ enters the contract with the bride and groom and guarantees that he will be present for them to help them be instruments of holiness for each other and to see that they have the strength and help they need as parents of a new family.

Marriage is also a church event because it is intended to exemplify and symbolize the love of Christ for his church. Catholic tradition invites us to look on the lifelong, faithful covenant of husband and wife as a symbol of the unchanging, ever faithful love of Christ for his community of faith.

Finally, marriage is a church event because of the role that married couples play in the life of the church. Our life in Christ that constitutes membership in the church is lived out on a day-to-day basis in the family. Parents are responsible for training their children in the fundamentals of the faith, and this happens in the context of family. That's why the church has taken to calling the family the "domestic church." The family is a basic unit of church life and is therefore important for the whole community of faith. That's why the foundational act of the family, officially entering the marriage relationship, must take place in the context of the church.

Given the involvement of Christ and the responsibilities that go along with married life, it's easy to see why those who are conscientious about their faith, that is, practicing Catholics, are anxious to make their marriage a church event.

The need for the church to be involved in the marriage of its members is so important that, if a Catholic enters a marriage "outside the church" (for example, in an exclusively civil ceremony), the marriage is not a sacrament. The couple may live together as husband and wife in the eyes of civil law, but they do so without an association with the church and, for that reason, they are not welcome to participate in the sacramental life of the church until their situation is regularized. It's not that the church wants to make things difficult for its members, but that the refusal of the couple to put the most important human association of their lives into the context of faith simply disqualifies them for the ordinary life of the church.

Given all this, it's easy to see why the church requires a certain amount of preparation for marriage. It is customary in many dioceses for those preparing for marriage to be given some personality tests to determine if there may be problems that they need to deal with before they carry their relationship any further. Then there are marriage instructions, sessions in which the couple learn, or recall, the church's teaching about the permanent nature of the sacrament of marriage, about the faithfulness and openness to children that is expected of those who enter the state of matrimony. Special questions arise if the couple is already living together before their wedding, questions about their intentions and about the probability of success in their marriage, and these questions have to be dealt with.

Here again, the church is not trying to make things difficult, but is trying to be sure that the bride and groom really understand what they are getting into. If it's not inappropriate to expect people to get some testing and training before they drive a car or fly an airplane, it's not inappropriate to expect people to get some testing and training for their marriage. It's a matter of the church's concern for the well-being of everybody: the spouses, their future families, the church at large.

The church is also concerned for the well-being of its members who have entered a marriage relationship outside the church context. When persons in such relationships want to return to the practice of the sacraments, it is necessary first to examine the situation in which they find themselves. Sometimes these situations are easy to "fix up" for example, if the parties were both free to marry but, for whatever reasons, did not come to the church to celebrate the sacrament of matrimony. Sometimes the situations are more complex, as when one or both parties have been in a previous marriage relationship. Then the church must examine those previous situations to determine whether there really was a marriage or whether there was some obstacle that made a true sacramental marriage impossible. For this purpose, dioceses have matrimonial tribunals in which these matters are considered and adjudicated. Most of the time parties are seeking what is called "a declaration of nullity," that is, a finding that their apparent past marriage was not a real and sacramental one and that they are therefore now free to enter into a sacramental union. Tribunals are not Catholic divorce courts, but rather an expression of the church's responsibility to uphold the seriousness of marriage.

The sacrament of matrimony, then, is not a simple and easy thing. It requires that those who would receive it be free of other marriage commitments and that they have the proper aptitudes, intentions and dispositions ahead of time. They have to go through the marriage instructions. Then comes what often seems the most difficult part of all: getting through the wedding and all of its surrounding challenges.

But that's only the beginning. There follows a lifetime together, a lifetime that generally brings a great deal of happiness to the husband and wife, but which also demands a kind of generosity and love that is unique to marriage. There are also the responsibilities that come with children, responsibilities of support and education and understanding. Having children involves a new level of self-sacrifice and, not rarely, anxiety. Once the children have grown, the marriage enters a new level as the spouses grow together into full maturity and old age. Marriage is complex and it requires continued presence and action on the part of the Lord as well as continued attention to the Lord on the part of the married persons if it is to be everything that it was meant to be.

Getting married is one thing. Being married is another. Getting married does not happen often in the lifetime of most people, and so it might not seem really appropriate to speak of it as a Catholic "practice," if a practice is something that we do over and over again. But being married is something that requires ongoing attentiveness, the habit of selflessness and, often, of forgiveness, and the practice of commitment and generosity. Practicing Catholics celebrate the inauguration of their marriage in the context of their faith and the faith of the Christian community, but they are also expected to live out their marriage, day by day and year by year, in that same context of the involvement of the Lord and the church in their married life. Faithful Christian marriage takes lots of practicing.

For Discussion and Reflection

• *What role have Christ and the church played in the marriages that you are most familiar with?*

• *What do people have the right to look for from the church when they get married?*

• *What makes a marriage happy?*

From the *Catechism of the Catholic Church*

Nos. 1621–1632; 1646–1657.

CHAPTER SEVEN

RAISING THE CHILDREN CATHOLIC

Good parents take care of their children. They look after their nourishment and clothing. They provide the love and stability that is vital to the children's present and future well-being. They see that the children get the best education that the family's circumstances can provide. Because parents are the instruments of God's providence for their children, they want to do everything they can for their offspring.

That's why parents who are practicing Catholics take pains to bring up their children in the faith. Catholic parents know that their religious faith is one of the most important things in their life, and they want to see that their children share that faith. It's one of the most precious things they have to hand on.

Their first responsibility in this context is to see that the children receive the sacrament of baptism. Baptism is the introduction of the life of Christ into our individual human existence. It is the door to church membership. It is the foundation on which everything else rests. Just as parents are responsible for the beginnings of their children's natural life, so they are responsible for their introduction into the life of faith. The church expects infants to be baptized within the first weeks after their birth (see canon 867).

Sometimes problems arise with the baptism of children. The priest learns that the parents are not regular in their practice of faith, that their membership in the church is not really important to them. Since baptism is the beginning of a relationship with God that calls for growth and development and nurturing, priests are unwilling to baptize children whose families do not seem to promise any support for the faith of the child. In these circumstances, the priest may deem it appropriate to delay the child's baptism for a while so he can help the parents renew their own religious commitment. This is not a matter of laying down a series of requirements for the parents to fulfill, but of helping them realize that baptism is more than a traditional religious observance that families with a past connection with the church go through.

Baptism, then, is the essential beginning, but it is only the beginning. Once the child has been baptized, the parents must see to it that the child gradually becomes involved in a whole complex of Catholic Christian religious acculturation and education.

Most important of all is that the children learn that faith is important in their lives, and the most ordinary way they learn this is by seeing that faith is important in the lives of their parents. Parents accomplish this to a great extent simply by being good practicing Catholics themselves. They show their children what it means to be Catholic by their own religious attitudes, by talking about what their faith means to them, by letting the children see that the faith of their parents is important enough to merit self-discipline and sacrifice. Children do pay attention to their parents, even when it may seem that they do not, and often parents teach their children much more than they themselves are aware of. Faith will be important in the family in which faith is important to the parents.

In this context, just being together is important. Sometimes one gets the impression that youngsters from contemporary families spend all their time elsewhere than at home, with people other than their parents and brothers and sisters. Maybe families have to work harder at being together than they used to, but without some regular and extended contact, education of the children in faith simply cannot take place.

But more than informal training in faith is called for. There have to be explicit attitudes and practices, too. In the home of practicing Catholics there will be prayers at meals and regular morning and evening prayers. The children will also know that praying is not just for kids, but something that their parents do, too. There will be crucifixes and religious pictures around the home expressing that the Lord and his saints are not far off somewhere but part of the ongoing life of the family. There may also be special ways in which the family observes Advent and Lent, Christmas and Easter, All Saints' Day and All Souls' Day, ways that highlight the presence and action of the Lord in the ongoing cycle of time.

Good parents will help their children learn that faith involves choices. What the children are allowed to see on TV or on the Internet, the words they use to refer to other people, the way their participation in organized sports is encouraged, the ideas of fairness, justice and care for the poor that they are presented with: All these are part of education in faith. They help the children learn that some behaviors and attitudes are acceptable to Catholic believers and that others are not. All good parents want to protect their children from wrong ideas about things like success, sexuality, violence, comfort and money. They do this most effectively not by preaching at their children, but by helping them form habits of making the right choices. Obviously, the choices that the parents make for themselves also have an important educational dimension for their children.

Then there is the question of formal religious education. Our Catholic faith is not just a matter of appropriate attitudes and practices. It also involves a vast body of teaching, of explicit principles and doctrines that Catholics need to be instructed in if their faith is to be something more than sentiment. Likewise, children need to learn that their faith extends beyond their homes, that other families are Catholic, too, that other children are also learning what it means to be a member of the community of faith.

Our Catholic schools are an immense help to parents in raising their children Catholic. They provide not just regular secular instruction, but organized instruction in Catholic teaching. They also offer moral training and socialization in the faith. They offer a kind of linkage between family religion and the knowledge and practice of Catholicism in the larger world. At a time when many of the values of society are so contrary to Catholic Christian values, our Catholic schools have a particularly important role to play in the education of future generations of practicing Catholics.

Not all parents send their children to Catholic schools, of course. Many are unable to do so for any number of reasons. But the need for formal education in the teachings of the church is still there. This is why parishes establish programs of religious education outside the context of school. Sometimes children are inclined to look on these programs as a nuisance, one more thing they are expected to do each week. Parents need to be wise enough to realize that these programs are a real service to their families, because they provide so many things that families are generally unable to provide for themselves and give their children opportunities to grow in faith in a bigger context. In view of that, parents will do everything they can to see that their children take advantage of what is offered.

One of the most basic principles of Catholic educational philosophy is that the parents are the primary educators of their children. This is why church leaders insist so regularly that parents ought to have some choice in the schools that are available for their children. But there is more to the principle than enabling parents to decide where their children are going to go to school. The primacy of the parents in education also means that the parents bear the primary responsibility in handing on Catholic faith and practice to their children. Nobody can adequately take their place. It is simply not right for parents to wash their hands of the religious training of their children once the children enter a Catholic school or begin to go to religious instruction classes.

Nobody can take full responsibility for the faith of somebody else, and often there is no accounting for why grown-up children do or do not practice their faith. But practicing Catholics know that they must do their best to pass on the treasure that they themselves have received.

For Discussion and Reflection
• *Who had the greatest influence on the early development of your faith?*
• *How can parents best encourage their children to treasure their faith?*
• *How can you help the children in your parish to practice and cherish Catholicism?*

From the *Catechism of the Catholic Church*
Nos. 2207–2213; 2221–2231.

CHAPTER EIGHT

BEING AN ACTIVE MEMBER OF A PARISH

All Catholics are members of a parish. You don't have to register. You don't have to make a financial pledge. Just by having a residence within a parish's territory, all those who have ever been members of the church, all those whose practice is irregular as well as all those who are at Mass every Sunday are members of the parish. All parish members have the right to orderly access to the sacraments, to preaching, to religious instruction, to pastoral care from the parish's ministers. Parish membership is not something for which people have to qualify. It's something that comes with their membership in the church.

But just as there is a distinction between belonging to the church and being practicing Catholics, so also there are those who are parish members and those who are active parish members. This chapter does not mean to suggest that those who are not active in their parish membership don't actually belong. But ongoing, week-by-week participation in the parish's life, that is, being an active member, is one of the important elements of being a practicing Catholic.

The parish (like the family) is a basic unit of church life for most people. They are married in a parish church, and their children are baptized in a parish church. They participate in the Eucharist there. Religious instruction comes to them through the parish. When they are sick, they are ministered to by representatives of the parish. When they die, they are buried from their parish. It is through the parish that most people relate to the full local church, the diocese and through the diocese to the church universal. It's only logical, therefore, that an active church life includes active involvement with the parish.

Most people belong to the parish in which they reside. In some dioceses, however, local diocesan legislation makes it possible for people to join a different parish if they choose to do so. There can be good reasons for this, such as convenience of transportation, or long-standing family connections, or special programs that are not available in the parish of residence. On the other hand, sometimes people will go to another parish just because they like the pastor there. But, whatever the reasons for going to another parish, membership in the parish of residence remains the norm, the regular way in which the church wants its members to be in touch with each other.

There are reasons for this. There is a certain "givenness" about parish life that is expressed by belonging just because you are there. The church universal is not a gathering of people who think exactly alike about everything, or prefer similar styles of preaching, or are all from a certain social class. The church universal is the community of all those who have been called to faith by Christ. So also, the parish is a more or less accidental mix of people brought together not by their preferences, but by their common life in the Lord Jesus. If "parish shopping" or self-selection becomes the norm, the church runs the risk of disintegrating into preferential enclaves of the elite, in which other persons may not feel welcome because they are not like everybody else. That sort of thing may be appropriate for a social club, but it is not appropriate for a parish.

Being active in parish membership means looking to the parish for the fulfillment of our ordinary spiritual needs: the Eucharist, the other sacraments and contact with the wider church. Because conscientious Catholics realize that these needs are ongoing, they are regular in their participation in their parish's life. They are eager to benefit from what the parish has to offer, and they have the right to expect that they will find what they need there.

But participation in parish life doesn't mean just going there to get what we need. It also means giving, and giving involves much more than regular contributions to the Sunday collection. Of course, parishes need financial resources to carry out their work, but the call to give extends further than giving money to pay the bills.

What we are called to give in our parish community is ourselves: our time, our talent, our presence, our counsel, our creativity, our concern for others, our encouragement and support of the parish leadership. Being part of a community means sharing responsibility for the life of the community.

This responsibility that we share is not just for the sake of the community's well-being, either. Of course, the parish needs the gifts that its members are able to provide, but more than that, the parishioners have a need to offer themselves for the well-being of the community. We need to give for the sake of our own well-being because sharing what we have is one of the most basic ways in which we express our gratitude for what we have been given.

Being diligent in the gift of ourselves to our parish is a logical consequence of our faith. Christ calls us to faith, not because we are deserving but because he is good. Christ makes us members of the church community, not because we have earned it but because he is generous. And the only appropriate response to generosity is generosity.

In the last decade or so, Catholic pastors have been encouraging stewardship. Stewardship is an approach to personal giving that suggests looking at what we have, not as our own possession, but as something entrusted to us by God. A steward is a trusted colleague of the master, to whom the master's resources have been committed, not for the well-being of the steward but for the purposes of the master. A good steward is one who makes use of what he or she has been given to further the master's wishes.

We remind ourselves of our dependence on God, and we express our role as God's stewards by consciously and deliberately sharing our time, our talent and our financial resources with others as agents of God's love for them. This sharing need not be confined exclusively to our parish, but a significant portion of the sharing should be directed there because it is in the parish that we most often and most explicitly experience God's love and concern for us.

Sometimes people wonder what kind of financial assistance they owe to their parish. A good rule of thumb is tithing, giving one tenth of our gross income to charitable purposes, half to the parish and the other half to other charitable causes. People who tithe often find that their generosity to their parish and other charitable works results in still further blessings from God, broader and deeper than what they have already been given.

Financial sharing is the easy part. Giving of our own selves is more difficult, especially in times of stress and uncertainty in the parish's life. It is, of course, possible to walk away when things get difficult in the parish and wait for things to quiet down. But walking away is hard to reconcile with gratitude and dedication.

The parish is one of the basic church contexts in which practicing Catholics express their faith. They are regular in their attendance at the Sunday parish Eucharist. They participate in the parish's educational and social programs. They pray for the sick and suffering of the parish. They are willing to lend a hand when they are asked, and even when they are not asked. Their faithfulness and generosity does not depend on their satisfaction with the way things are going at any given time. By their willingness to receive and to share in the parish, they encourage and deepen the faith of all of its members as well as their own.

The reason the church "assigns" each one of us to a parish community is that we need community in order to be Catholic. Our faith can't survive without it.

The church also assigns each one of us to a parish because we need a context in which to contribute to the faith of others. They need our presence and our participation.

Practicing Catholics look on their parish as their home because they know that that's where they belong. And they know that home is not just a place to receive but also a place to give. That's why they are active parishioners.

For Discussion and Reflection
• *How are you active in your parish?*
• *What would happen in a parish if nobody but the priest needed to be active?*
• *What does your parish mean to you?*

From the *Catechism of the Catholic Church*
Nos. 2179; 2226.

CHAPTER NINE

OFFERING IT UP

Some time ago, a surgeon friend of mine was doing local surgery on a retired nun. She was not having an easy time. "Oh, it hurts. I need a drink of water. I don't think I can go on with this. I'm going to be sick." The surgeon was not happy with this and finally said in desperation, "Oh, Sister, just offer it up."

Whenever I tell this story to lifetime Catholics, they chuckle because "offering it up" strikes such a familiar chord in their Catholic memory. We remember being told by the sisters who taught us in school (as well as by our parents and grandparents) to "offer it up" when we had to miss the Christmas party or when we scraped our knee on the playground or when the school cafeteria served food that we didn't like. All the little trials of life seemed to elicit the same advice: "Offer it up."

Yet "offering it up" is not just an expedient for getting through childhood. "Offering it up" is an important part of practicing our faith throughout our life, and it involves not just trials and tribulations but gifts and blessings as well.

Many Catholics pray the Morning Offering as part of the beginning of each day: "O Jesus, through the Immaculate Heart of Mary, I offer You the prayers, works, joys, and sufferings of this day...." Even as adults, they are still "offering it up."

Deliberately presenting to God the events of our daily life is a way of keeping ourselves conscious that our life is not an accidental chain of meaningless happenings, nor something that is of significance to ourselves alone. "Offering it up" is a way of expressing our awareness of the presence and action of God in our lives. Giving our joys and sorrows to God involves a realization that they come from him, that he is somehow involved in them, that they are part of God's providence for our lives, that some dimension of everything that happens in our lives is a gift that we are called to acknowledge by sharing it with him in gratitude.

The joys of our life are easy to offer back to God because we seem to understand them more easily. When we get a raise in our salary or run into a friend that we haven't seen for a long time or find that something we have said has been helpful to somebody else or successfully bring a project to completion, it's easy to be grateful. It's easy to believe that God has been at work in these circumstances of our life. It's easy to present the gift back in gratitude to God's kindness and to acknowledge that it belongs to him as much as it belongs to us.

Of course, even this requires a certain level of attentiveness because we are all inclined to take good things for granted, to think we deserve them, or to believe that they result from our efforts alone. We have to cultivate the habit of awareness of God's part in our lives, the habit of gratitude, and cultivating habits requires practice. Practicing Catholics strive to be habitually grateful for the obvious blessings they discover in their lives and to offer them back to the Lord.

Other things are less easy to offer up. The sudden death of a loved one, a serious illness, severe financial problems, mistreatment from a colleague, ongoing tension in a marriage: These are grave and painful matters, and it's often hard to see how they could possibly be part of God's care for us or how God could be pleased by receiving them from us as an offering. But Catholics offer these things up, too.

Spiritual writers speak of the "mystery" of suffering, in part because suffering doesn't admit of easy explanations. But it's important to realize that, in a Christian context, "mystery" is not merely something we find hard to understand, but also an ongoing revelation of God's loving providence for us.

In order to come to grips with the mystery of suffering in our lives, we have to look to the mystery of suffering in the life of Jesus.

Here was a man who was totally virtuous, totally without sin, totally dedicated to doing the will of God, who yet suffered misunderstanding and scorn and rejection, who was abandoned by his friends, and who was put to death as a common criminal. Yet his was the life that brought redemption to all humankind, not because it was a life of suffering, but because the suffering was a result of his faithfulness to God and was accepted by him as a consequence of that faithfulness.

Jesus saved us by demonstrating to us what faithfulness can involve, by making up for the unfaithfulness of others (including ourselves) and by enabling us, through faith, to participate in and extend his life of self-giving and dedication to the Father through our own life.

What does the life of Jesus teach us about the mystery of suffering? For one thing, it teaches us that suffering is not always a punishment. Sometimes we do bring our sufferings on ourselves, but pain and sorrow also come to the innocent, as they came to Jesus, and when they come to us, it doesn't necessarily mean that God is trying to repay us for wrongdoing or that we are immediately responsible for everything that happens to us.

The life of Jesus also teaches us that suffering is not just suffering, a necessary but meaningless element in ordinary human existence. There can be significance to suffering, as there was significance to the suffering of Jesus. The suffering we experience as Christian believers, therefore, is not just a negative interlude in our individual existence, but somehow a sharing in the experience of Christ, whose life we share. Our task is not to understand it but to accept it in faith and then let God work out how it all fits together.

Finally, the life and suffering of Jesus also teach us that we do not suffer alone. Because Christ shares the life of all those who have faith in him, the pain of the individual believer is also somehow the pain of Christ. He unites our suffering to his. Then, too, the patience and faith-filled dedication with which the individual believer bears his or her suffering also contribute something to the lives of all the others who share the life of Christ. Somehow, our faithful suffering strengthens the well-being of the whole community of faith.

All that having been said, suffering is still painful and perplexing. It is still a mystery. That's why we offer it up. We don't fully understand the reason for it or its details. We don't rejoice in it. We don't welcome it. We merely present it to God in faith, hope and love with the confidence that the life of Christ is somehow at work here and that, just as his suffering brought grace and redemption to the world, so also our suffering will somehow contribute to our life and happiness and to the life and happiness of those who share his life with us.

The alternatives to offering up our sufferings with and to the suffering Christ are self-pity, bitterness, ongoing confusion and a lack of meaning and depth in our lives. We can try to rebel against it, we can grit our teeth and just get through it, or we can invite the Lord to make it for us an occasion of increase in faith and peace for ourselves and for others, something worth offering to him.

"Offering it up" is more than a Catholic catchphrase, a bit of cultural slang, a superficial throwaway line that implies not paying attention to things we cannot change. Offering up the works and joys and sufferings of our life means consciously contributing them to the ongoing life of Christ and to the life of all those who share the life of Christ. It is a deliberate way of assimilating and expressing the meaning that our faith offers us in all the facets of our lives.

"Offering it up" is not something that comes to us automatically, even after the years of conditioning that some of us had from the sisters, priests and brothers in Catholic schools. It requires thought, prayer, patience and practice. But it's an important element in being a practicing Catholic.

For Discussion and Reflection

• *What do you have to "offer up" in your life?*

• *Does offering up something make a difference in the way you look at it?*

• *What blessings have you received through suffering?*

From the *Catechism of the Catholic Church*

Nos. 618; 2031; 2100.

CHAPTER TEN

BEING IN TOUCH WITH MARY
AND THE SAINTS

People who are not Catholic sometimes wonder about Catholics' devotion to the Blessed Virgin Mary and the other saints. Catholic churches generally contain pictures and statues of Mary and the saints, often with vigil lights burning in front of them. Catholics will talk about their patron saints, or about praying to Saint Anthony when they have lost something. Sometimes they go on pilgrimage to Fatima or Lourdes or to the shrine of Saint Anne de Beaupre in Canada. Occasionally, it seems that Catholics are more at home with the saints than they are with the Lord.

Being in touch with Mary and the saints is one of the distinguishing elements of the Catholic culture. It's an important part of being a practicing Catholic. There are several fundamental insights behind Catholic devotion to the saints.

First of all, we are dealing with a kind of family matter here. Being Catholic means being in a family, and being in a family means having relatives. Our relatives as members of the church include not only our brother Jesus, but all his brothers and sisters as well. Most of these brothers and sisters are pretty much the same as we are, ordinary people without anything special to recommend them—except their membership in the family. Others are quite special, the really successful members of the family to whom we others look with particular affection and regard. These are the ones we call the saints. Practicing Catholics are generally attentive to their relatives.

Implicit in this family attentiveness is the conviction that the saints are not just figures from history that we look back on with admiration and gratitude. They are still alive with and in the Risen Lord in heaven. Their life continues, although in a form that is different from their earthly existence. And because our life of faith is also a sharing in the life of the Risen Christ, we are in contact with the Lord's saints in and through him.

But that's not all. Just as we are in touch with the saints through the life of Jesus that we share, so they are in touch with us. They love us in him and care for us in him. They don't look down on us from heaven as detached spectators of what's going on here in our lives, but as our brothers and sisters who are looking out for those they love. Just as the life and love of Jesus is expressed and extended on earth by those who live in faith, so also the life and love of Jesus is expressed and extended from heaven by those who live in glory. Just as the family of the Lord is not limited by place, but extends throughout the earth, so also the family of the Lord is not limited by time and by the presence of its members in earthly life.

Catholic devotion to Mary and the other saints and Catholic confidence in the intercession and help of the saints for us are ways in which we express our family awareness and loyalty. Being Catholic is never a matter of just me and Jesus. It's always we and Jesus, and the "we" includes Mary, the Mother of God, and all the other saints. We're all part of the same family. We somehow all belong together.

The most honored of the saints is Mary, the Mother of God. Mary is, in many ways the original saint because she came to know and accept Jesus first of all. She shared his life from beginning to end and now occupies a special place with him in heaven. Because of her special place in the earthly and risen life of Jesus, she has a special place in the Lord's family. Because she is Jesus' mother, she is everybody else's mother, too.

Catholics pray to Mary under many different titles: Mother of Mercy, Mother of Good Counsel, Refuge of Sinners, Queen of Peace. In fact, there is a special prayer, the Litany of the Blessed Mother, which contains nearly fifty different titles under which Mary is invoked. This richness of address indicates the breadth and variety of

Mary's virtues. It also indicates that Catholics look on Mary in many different lights, under many aspects, depending on our state at any given time and the needs for which we are asking her help. Mary's many titles also suggest that there is so much to admire and imitate about our mother that one way of speaking of her simply isn't enough.

Then there are the other saints, almost without number. One of the learned works on the saints runs to twelve large volumes, and a handbook that gives special attention to saints of the English-speaking world runs to 514 pages and contains about 1,500 entries. There are all kinds of saints: popes and bishops and priests, laywomen and men, religious sisters and brothers and monks. There are saints that were kings and emperors and saints who were beggars; saints who astounded the world with their learning and saints who couldn't read and write. Perhaps one of the most fascinating factors of this great family to which we belong is its variety. You don't have to be of a certain personality type to be a saint. You don't have to come from a certain country. You don't have to have undertaken a certain prescribed set of religious practices. The one thing that all saints have in common, both those who have been officially declared saints by the church through the process of canonization and the other citizens of heaven who have not received official attention, is their love for the Lord Jesus and their dedication to him. Given that, the only limits to the variety of the saints are the limits of human diversity.

That's probably why every Catholic has his or her own favorite saints. Some saints seem more attractive to us because we find them somehow like ourselves. Perhaps they were interested in the same things we find interesting, or they had to deal with some of the same crosses that we carry. Most of us know something about the saints whose names we received in baptism or confirmation, and we like to think that they are especially interested in us.

Then there are the specialists, those who, for some reason or other, have been approached by Catholic believers over the centuries in times of special need or in particular circumstances: Saint Luke, the patron of physicians; Saint Francis de Sales, the patron of authors; Saint Lucy for diseases of the eyes; Saint Dymphna for mental disorders; Saint Francis of Assisi, patron of ecologists; and, of course, Saint Anthony for finding things that we have lost. They are all part of the family, like favorite aunts or cousins, and they are all interested in the other members of the family.

Catholics express their devotion to Mary and the saints in many different ways. They offer prayers to them. They visit their statues in churches, sometimes lighting a vigil candle to represent their needs. They treat them with a certain degree of familiarity: "I'll have to talk to Saint Jude about that."

Many Catholics are able to visit the shrines of the saints, particular places where devotion is expressed in a special way. Often people look on shrines as places you go to get cured of illness. Lourdes, for example, is a sanctuary of the Blessed Mother that is much frequented by sick people. But when people visit shrines, even though they may have their own special agenda, they also realize that the Blessed Mother or the saint may respond to their prayers in ways other than what they expect. Not everyone who visits Lourdes comes home cured, but there are few who leave there without some sense of healing and a deepened understanding of the Lord's action in their lives.

Catholics do not offer the same kind of reverence to the saints that they offer to God. The saints can never take the place of Jesus, precisely because it is the life of Jesus that constitutes the common element that keeps the family together. Without him, there would be no family. But there is a family, his family of faith and glory, and when Catholics pay their respects to Mary and the saints, they are offering their respect also to the One in whom the family has its origin.

Practicing Catholics are comfortable in the company of the saints. It's one of the ways they express their attachment to their family.

For Discussion and Reflection

• *Who are your favorite saints? Why?*
• *How do you express your attachment to Mary and the other saints?*
• *How does being in touch with the saints help you?*

From the *Catechism of the Catholic Church*

Nos. 971; 954–959.

CHAPTER ELEVEN

BEING WILLING TO BE DIFFERENT

In the middle of the second century, an anonymous author wrote a letter to a man named Diognetus in which he describes the situation of Christian believers in the pagan world:

> Christians are not distinguishable from others either by nationality, language, or custom. They don't inhabit separate cities of their own, or speak a strange dialect. With regard to dress, food, and manner of life in general, they follow the customs of whatever city they happen to be living in. And yet there is something extraordinary about their lives. They live in their own countries as though they were only passing through. Any country can be their homeland, but for them their homeland, wherever it may be, is a foreign country. We may say that the Christian is to the world what the soul is to the body. As the soul is present in every part of the body, while remaining distinct from it, so Christians are found in all cities of the world, but cannot be identified with the world. (*Letter to Diognetus,* chapter 5 and following)

Things haven't changed much since the second century. Being a believer today means that we may seem to be just like everybody else but, in fact, we are different. It's important for practicing Catholics to be conscious of where the difference lies and to be willing to embrace it.

Of course, there are some obvious and visible differences in the lives of practicing Catholics, aspects of their life that set them apart from other people and identify them as Catholics.

When you see somebody make the Sign of the Cross and say a meal prayer in a restaurant, for example, you know that that person is probably a Catholic. If the neighbors go to Mass on Sunday, send their children to the parish school and have a statue of the Blessed Mother in their living room, they are almost certainly Catholics because they do Catholic things. That's how you can tell.

But these identifiably "Catholic things" don't make them all that much different from the other people on the street. They wear the same kinds of clothes as everybody else, drive the same kind of car and take the same kind of vacations. There doesn't seem to be anything extraordinary about their life. Yet, if they are really practicing Catholics, there is something that is quite different about them. It's their values and their priorities.

Being practicing Catholics means having a whole system of values that are different from the values of many, perhaps most of the people around them. This system of values helps them determine what is important in their lives and what is secondary, what they are going to stand up for and what they are going to overlook. The way they deal with their jobs and their families, their use of time and money will be determined by these values and the relationship between the values. Practicing Catholics are people with definite and clear priorities, and often their priorities are different from those of other people.

The top priority for a believer is the life of Christ. As baptized persons, we have been given a share of the life of Jesus. Together with all the other believers in the world (as well as the saints in heaven) we are called and empowered to receive the life and love of Jesus in our hearts and to extend that life and love to those around us: our family, our friends, our neighbors, our colleagues at work. That's what the life of a Christian believer is all about, and that's what is more important than anything else.

Consequently, maintaining, strengthening and responding to the life of Christ in us takes precedence over everything else. That's why practicing Catholics go to Mass on Sunday. That's why they receive the sacraments and pray. That's why they take pains with the religious education of their children. It's all part of living in Christ Jesus.

Our life in Christ, however, doesn't determine only our specifically religious behavior. It also offers us a whole set of principles and attitudes about the other aspects of our life. The way we think about success and failure, the way we look on other people, especially those in need, the significance we find in civic and political life, the way we view sickness and death: All of these matters are colored by the life of Jesus that is in us. In fact, every aspect of our human existence involves some connection with the life of the Lord.

These principles and attitudes, which arise from our relationship with Jesus, guide just about every decision that practicing Catholics are asked to make. What kind of employment will we accept, and how far are we willing to go to comply with what is asked of us in our work? To what extent do we respond to our consumer culture that keeps telling us to buy and use and throw away and buy some more? How important is it for the children to be on the soccer team? Do we watch the same TV programs as everybody else? Our lives are full of decisions, and those decisions are made on the basis of some sort of values, conscious or unconscious. For the practicing Catholic, there is no question about what the values must be: They must be the values of Christ, the values that Christ offers us through his church.

These values are not necessarily the values of the world around us. We may not live in a militantly pagan world as Diognetus did, where being a Christian could cost you your life, but there is enough around us to make it clear that we are living in a spiritually foreign land. Human life, that basic gift of God, has been cheapened to the point that people feel free to kill their own unborn children. Human success is measured in bank accounts and fame rather than in generosity and self-sacrifice. Human worth has to be proved rather than assumed. Human commitments like marriage are vulnerable to being dissolved when one of the parties decides it's time for a change. We are invited to believe that we are supposed to be comfortable at every moment and that even a headache is somehow unfair. The values and assumptions behind all this, the principles on which our world operates are different from the values and principles of Christ and his church. Consequently, people who accept the values of Christ are often out of step with the rest of the world. They are different, even as Christ was.

The difference, however, does not lead believers to try to get out of the world or to set up enclaves of safety in which they will not need to be involved in it. In fact, the life of Christ in believers impels them to love the world as he did. It's a good world, deep down, because it's God's world. That's why Jesus came to save it, to give it a new value and a new worth through participation in his life. Our task as believers is to bring the world that life, just as the soul brings life to the body. We may not be high-level decision makers or influential guides of public opinion. We may not be important at all, as the world counts importance. But we do have a part to play in the world's salvation, and we play that part by being as consistently, as completely, as practically Christian as our opportunities allow.

Practicing Catholics are people with priorities, the Lord's priorities. They don't necessarily parade their priorities around and make speeches about them, but the priorities are there, and they influence the lives of practicing Catholic believers in lots of different ways. Some of the ways are obvious to anyone who wants to observe them. Some of the ways are more subtle and are clear only to people who choose to look carefully. Some of the ways in which Christian priorities have their effect in the believer's life are known only to the Lord. But the priorities are there, and they are operative.

They are not the priorities that are shared by many of the people around us. We may seem to be just like everybody else in many ways, but in the ways that make the most difference to ourselves and to the world around us, we are different. Being a practicing Catholic means understanding and welcoming the difference.

For Discussion and Reflection

• *What do you value most in your life?*

• *Have you ever had to be conspicuously different because you are a Catholic?*

• *In what ways do you bear witness to your faith?*

From the *Catechism of the Catholic Church*

Nos. 816; 2044–2046; 2471–2473.

CHAPTER TWELVE

DYING CATHOLIC

Dying Catholic is as much a part of Catholic practice as is living Catholic. It's not that we individually do it often, of course! Yet the way we die, the context of the end of our lives is determined by the whole practice of our lives. At the same time, it is not just our own individual death that is important, but also the way we relate to and participate in the deaths of other people. That, too, is part of being a practicing Catholic.

The world in which we live, from which Catholics are different in so many ways, doesn't like to deal with death. It doesn't even like to use the word but finds other ways of referring to it. In our secular culture death has become a biological embarrassment, to be gotten through as quickly, quietly and painlessly as possible, with a minimum of muss, fuss and bother.

Catholics look on death both as the final statement or act of a precious human life on earth and as the passage to a fuller, final life with the Risen Christ in heaven. As the first preface for the Mass for Christian Death puts it, "The sadness of death gives way to the bright promise of immortality" and "life is changed, not ended."

There are particular external expressions of membership in the community of faith that are called for at the end of earthly life just as there are for other moments of life. Practicing Catholics want these expressions of faith to be part of their own dying and provide them for their loved ones when they die.

The first of these is the sacrament of the anointing of the sick. The celebration of this sacrament is not limited to the last moments of life, but offers the healing and strengthening action of Christ and the prayers of his church to all who begin to be in danger of death from sickness, from old age or in the context of a serious operation. This sacrament is intended to increase our faith, hope and love at a time when fear and confusion could otherwise turn our attention away from God.

But if the sacrament of the anointing of the sick is given to all those who suffer from serious illness and infirmity, it is particularly appropriate for those who are at the point of departing this life. In that circumstance, it is usually accompanied by the sacrament of reconciliation and the reception of Holy Communion as *viaticum*, food for the journey. Practicing Catholics let their relatives and friends know that they wish to receive these "last rites" when their own life is coming to an end, and they take pains to see that these rites are accessible to those for whom they share responsibility. They know that God wants to be with his faithful when they are sick and dying, even as he wants to be with them in the rest of their life.

The death of the Christian believer is followed by the funeral. The order of Christian funerals ordinarily has three parts. The first is the vigil, which generally takes place at a funeral home but can also be carried out in the church where the funeral liturgy will take place. This rite is a series of readings and prayers which are intended to help the dead person's family and friends express their sorrow and find strength and consolation in their faith in Christ and his resurrection. Other members of the Christian community offer support to the mourners by being present and by praying that the one they have lost may have eternal life.

Next is the funeral Mass. At this eucharistic celebration the community of faith offers the sacrifice of Christ together not just for the eternal rest of the one who has died, but also as an expression of the link between the death of the believer and the death and resurrection of Jesus. Funeral Masses generally include a homily. The funeral homily is not intended to be a eulogy of the dead person (which is more appropriate as part of the vigil service or the final commendation), but rather an instruction based on sacred Scripture about the Christian significance of life and death and about the meaning of the death and resurrection of Jesus. The participants at the funeral Mass are invited to receive Holy Communion, not only to pray for the deceased in their moments with the Lord, but also to express their faith in the eternal life that we all hope to share with the Risen Christ. After a brief commendation ceremony, in which the body is generally incensed as a sign of honor to the dead person's dignity as a member of Christ, the mourners proceed to the cemetery for the rite of committal.

At the cemetery, there are further prayers and the body is committed to its grave, the final act of the community of faith caring for the body of its deceased member. At the end, the presiding minister invites the participants to "Go in peace," an invitation that they have heard in many other contexts but which has a special meaning in the context of the peace they have been seeking for their dear one.

In the past, it was not permitted for Catholics to have their body cremated, since cremation was generally used as a sign that the dead person did not believe in eternal life. Now cremation is permitted, but traditional burial is generally preferred as being more in accord with the long practice of the church and as a clearer sign of Catholics' belief in the final resurrection. Most Catholics want to be buried in a Catholic cemetery as a last sign of their attachment to and gratitude for the community of faith in which they spent their lives.

It's important for Catholics to understand what a funeral is really all about. It is not intended to be an accolade of respectability for a life well lived but an expression of care from Christ and the church for a member whose earthly journey is now ended. Criminals and saints, popes and paupers, people who went to Mass every day and people who haven't practiced their faith in years can be "buried from the church." All Catholics (as well as catechumens) have the right to a Catholic funeral. You don't have to qualify, as long as you have been somehow in touch with the church at some point in your life. The point is not that how one has lived or how faithful one has been is of no significance to God and the church. The point is that judgment is the prerogative of the Lord and that, when the end comes, we must all rely on the kindness and mercy of the Lord.

The way we die and the way we observe the death of others reflect a whole attitude toward life and the value of life. It's part of a Catholic consistency that includes attitudes toward terrible things like abortion and assisted suicide and wonderful things like family, friendship and community in the Lord. Catholics don't believe that you have to cling to life with every conceivable means or that death is the worst thing that could happen to us. They see life as a gift on loan from God that they must care for with good human prudence and use as productively as they can. And when that life comes to an end, they look forward to something even better.

Having a Catholic funeral is a statement, a statement about faith and hope on the part of the dead person, or at least on the part of his or her family, and on the part of the church. It expresses who we are and what we hope to become. It expresses something about the significance of each and every human life, and in so doing, offers hope for the one who has died and authentic Christian comfort for those who remain behind.

After the Second Vatican Council, the church's funeral liturgy changed. Before, the liturgy stressed loss and the prospect of judgment. Those elements are not denied in the present liturgy, but they are balanced by a greater sense of God's love and mercy. That's why priests are permitted to wear white vestments now as well as black or purple. A funeral is not an occasion of undiluted grief but an occasion of gratitude, comfort and hope. That's why practicing Catholics want their death to be observed in the context of the community of the church and why they make provision for the church's participation in the death of those they love.

For Discussion and Reflection

• *Are you afraid of death? Why? Why not?*
• *What do you think about when you go to a funeral?*
• *How are you preparing for your death?*

From the *Catechism of the Catholic Church*

Nos. 1010–1014; 1520–1523; 1681–1690.

CONCLUSION

Being a practicing Catholic has to do with Jesus in our lives. It is the way we respond to and express two basic principles that were inherent in the life and ministry of Jesus and which continue to be operative in his church: the incarnational principle and the sacramental principle.

The incarnational principle is that in Jesus God became a human being, a true and full human being with body and soul, with temptations and frustrations, with emotions and bodily pains. Only sin was missing in his human existence. Through the Incarnation, God became a participant in human space and in human time. By means of the human nature that he took on, Jesus redeemed the world. Since the Incarnation, the world is God's world in a way that it had not been before. But the Incarnation is not over. Jesus is still true God and true man, still active in our world, still offering us redemption. God still loves us today as he loved us during the time of Jesus' earthly ministry. The action of Father and Son continues through the Holy Spirit in the church. The church is not God, but it is the chief instrument of God's ongoing activity all around us. The church works through its members, which means that those who strive to be active in their faith are both recipients and instruments of God's redeeming action in the world. They benefit from and extend the incarnational activity of Jesus.

The sacramental principle is a parallel to the incarnational principle. Just as Jesus uses his humanity and ours to bring about his saving activity, so also he uses other created things, things like bread, wine, water and words, to initiate and sustain his life in us. Practicing Catholics understand and appreciate the sacramental nature of Jesus' activity in the seven canonical sacraments of the church. But the sacramental principle is also operative in the words of the church's ministers, in the blessings that come to believers through their families and friends, in "ordinary" things like sunsets, rainstorms and the quiet passages of time.

Being a practicing Catholic is not a matter of going through a complicated series of special motions in order to keep God aware of us, but of engaging in a whole style of life that will keep us aware of God, receptive to what God is giving us, attentive to what God entrusts to us to hand on to others. It means being conscious of and responsive to the presence and action of the Lord in the church, in ourselves and in the world around us. It means taking seriously both the incarnational principle and the sacramental principle. This is what lies behind the practices that I have described here.

Not all the practices are equally important. Raising the children Catholic is more important than praying to the saints, and participating in the life of the parish is more important than saying the litany of the Blessed Mother.

The fundamental Catholic practices are the sacraments, those extensions of the incarnational activity of Jesus that are expressed in the words and actions that he entrusted to his church for our salvation. The sacraments are not "things" that we receive but events in which we participate. These events bring the action of Christ to bear on the special occasions of our life, like birth and marriage and death, but they also sanctify our earthly existence day to day and week to week. A believer who is out of touch with the sacraments is not a practicing Catholic because he or she has lost contact with those actions of the Lord that imbue our lives with his presence and make them Catholic Christian lives.

There are many other Catholic practices that I have not treated in these reflections, things like novenas and the Way of the Cross and the observance of First Fridays. These practices, and others like them, are matters of personal choice and taste. Every practicing Catholic has his or her own mix of observances that, together with the essential ones, constitute a personalized way of living out the faith. But all authentic Catholic practice is somehow rooted in the principles of incarnation and sacramentality that lie at the heart of our Catholic existence.

Just as there are different styles of Catholic practice, so there are different levels of intensity. Some practicing Catholics content themselves with the minimum, observing only the specific demands of church law. Others are more fervent. They go to Mass during the week, take on greater penitential practices during Lent and are active and generous in the life of their parish. Obviously, a deeper and more developed level of practice is better both for the individual church member and for the church community at large. Being content with the minimum is to settle for survival. The Lord invites us to more than that.

Sometimes new devotions or observances arise in the church, new ways of praying or new emphases on old truths or new manifestations of the action of the Blessed Mother or the saints. Church authorities are generally slow to offer their approval to such things because it takes time to determine whether they are wholesome and authentic or not. Catholics are free to respond to such movements as part of their faith practice as long as these new developments have not been explicitly rejected by the church, but it is always clear that such new developments cannot substitute for or supersede the basics of Catholic practice, such as doing penance and participating in the sacraments.

Our Catholic faith is a gift. It is an invitation from God to share in the life of his incarnate Son Jesus. And it calls for a response. There is the response of basic acceptance in baptism through which we begin to live the life of Christ and become members of the church forever. But that's not enough. Our lives change and develop day by day, and our response to God's gift of faith has to be a day-by-day response. That response is constituted by our practice of the faith. Through our habits of prayer and participation in the sacraments, through the way we live our family life, through the conscious way we deal with the blessings and the burdens of our life, through the manner in which we carry out our responsibilities to the Christian community around us, through all this we are responding to God's gift to us of his own life.

Practicing our faith is not just a way of maintaining our identity in a traditional Catholic subculture. It's not a mechanism to earn God's benevolence. It is an ongoing response to God's generosity. And if the response is not made, the generosity will be taken for granted, under-appreciated and soon forgotten.

But that's not all. Our response to God's generosity in the practice of our faith is not just necessary for our individual ongoing spiritual health and vitality. Other people need our response, too. The other members of the community of faith need the example of our response as an encouragement to their own. The simple fact of being with other believers on Sunday strengthens the faith of everybody who is there. The dedication of one Catholic family enriches the life of the Catholic family next door.

But it's not just a matter of example. Because the community of faith is an extension of the one life of the Risen Christ, the energy and commitment of each member strengthen the whole Body. The church needs the faithful practice of its members for the sake of its own corporate well-being and energy.

Finally, the benefit of our practice is not just limited to other believers. We are all called to spread the gospel. You don't have to write books or preach sermons to do that. Simply letting other people see in our practice what our faith means to us is an invitation to them to share it and therefore a blessing for them.

In the last analysis, being a practicing Catholic means living consistently with what we are: ordinary men and women called to share and express the life of the Risen Christ as a matter of practice.

For Discussion and Reflection

• *How has the Catholic practice of others been a blessing in your life?*

• *To what extent are you a practicing Catholic?*

• *How long has it been since you have received the sacraments?*

From the *Catechism of the Catholic Church*

Nos. 519–521; 738–740; 949–953.

PART THREE
THINKING CATHOLIC

INTRODUCTION

It is clear that the world around us doesn't give the kind of support to Catholic Christian belief and behavior that it once did, and that living a Christian life is therefore harder than it used to be.

In our American society people used to agree without a second thought that abortion was criminal, that divorce was bad, that sexual activity outside of marriage was wrong, that homosexual behavior was not natural. Today all of these things are not only acceptable in our culture but are, in fact, looked upon as rights that no one can take away. That's the message that is conveyed to us over and over again in popular music, movies and TV programs. All we have to do is read the daily papers (and their advertisements) to realize that the values many people hold are not Christian values such as self-sacrifice and patience and obedience to the will of the Lord.

Our American society is dedicated to consumption. We are bombarded with invitations to buy, to enjoy, to use up, to throw away and then to buy again. While many voices tell us why to buy certain products, there seem to be few voices that tell us the purpose of all this buying and using up. Our whole country seems to be engaged in an activity that nobody can really justify. It's an exercise in futility.

Equally shallow are many of the commonly accepted ideas about success, work, comfort, education and human relationships.

From the point of view of a believer, none of it makes much sense. The world seems to have gone crazy.

If we are to maintain our Catholic Christian faith in the midst of all this madness, we have to be able to maintain our equilibrium. We have to have something inside of us that helps us keep our balance when everything around us seems to be sliding toward dissolution.

Knowledge is important. We need to know what God asks us to believe and do. We also need to understand that the real demands of our faith are not the whims of a difficult God, but guidance about authentic growth and development.

Knowledge is important, but it is not enough. If it were, straight A's in religion and theology courses ought to guarantee faithfulness and virtue in religious belief and practice, but they don't. Something more than knowledge seems to be called for.

This "something more" is what I call "thinking Catholic." Thinking Catholic is not just a matter of knowing what Christ and his church teach, even in detail. Thinking Catholic is a mindset, an attitude of the heart, a bundle of insights and presumptions and priorities and directions that are derived from faith and which, in turn, strengthen and vitalize the practice of faith. Catholic thinking is like a hidden file in a computer program that may never appear on the screen but that governs the whole operation of the program. If it is not there, things just are not going to work.

The people who think Catholic are those who are able to maintain their sense of equilibrium in a crazy world. Those who do not are sucked into the whirlpool, no matter how much they may have been taught about the specifics of Catholic faith and practice.

These insights, presumptions and priorities that lie in the heart of the faithful believer are concerned with God and the world, with life and living, with suffering and sin, with the individual and the family and with society at large. They involve our attitudes toward happiness, toward knowledge and the arts, toward the inconsistencies of human existence. Thinking Catholic includes our attitudes toward Christ and prayer and the church.

Thinking Catholic is not something we can outline with completeness and detail because it contains so many elements and because it is as complex as the human heart. It is a mixture of motivating forces that may vary from individual to individual, but that includes some essential features common to all faithful believers. It is not a collection of separate items like tools in a toolbox, but rather a blend of energies, each of which influences the others, like the various flavors in good wine.

In the chapters that follow, I offer a description of thinking Catholic. I use the word *description* deliberately because I am sure that others would be able to find other aspects of the Catholic mindset or explain differently the ones I present. I will deal with what I perceive.

I will treat the elements of thinking Catholic that have to do with the world around us, then those concerned with our life and how we live it. I will then have something to say about aspects of thinking Catholic that govern our relationship with the church and our religious practice. This may involve a modicum of repetition of matters of which we have already spoken. Moreover, because the Catholic mindset is a matter of general attitudes rather than specific teachings and practices, I have not included references to the *Catechism of the Catholic Church* in this part of *Being Catholic*.

My purpose here is not polemic. I have not set out to demonstrate how crazy and how bad things are in the world that surrounds us. There isn't much need for such a demonstration. Those who need to be convinced that things are not what they should be have only to consider the frenzy and the frustration of the world's "successful" people to see that the world promises more than it can deliver, that its sales pitch is tinged with madness.

My purpose is to clarify the Catholic heart and the Catholic mind to show how deeply different we are—or should be—from many of those around us. It is my hope that becoming aware of what lies within the heart of those who think Catholic will enable those who read these reflections to become aware of the richness that both derives from our faith and also energizes it. This awareness may be of some assistance in staying faithful in a crazy world. I will be grateful to the Lord if these reflections help people to savor, appreciate and nourish the gift of thinking Catholic.

CHAPTER ONE

A WONDERFUL WORLD

How we look on the world pretty well determines how we see everything else in our lives. If we see the world as a result of some cosmic fluke, we will see our own lives as fundamentally meaningless, to be lived out as comfortably and pleasantly as we can make them until the time comes for the end of our absurd existence. If we see the world as a grim and desolate place, we will expect to lead grim and desolate lives. If we see the world as a place of trial and temptation in which God is constantly exercising quality control over the creatures that have been placed here, we will see everything as threat and live our lives in cowering fear. If we see the world exclusively as a vale of tears, we will see everything as a cause for lamentation.

Most people don't seem to give much thought to the nature and meaning of the universe. They leave such questions to scientists and philosophers. Instead, they take life as it comes, one day at a time, pursuing their various inclinations and generally following the path of least resistance. But in living that way, they are nonetheless implicitly saying something about their view of the world. They are saying that it really isn't very important, just as their own lives are unimportant to anyone beyond themselves and their immediate circle of human contacts.

The best way to look at the world is through the eyes of the One who put it here in the first place. At the beginning of the Bible, we learn that God thinks the world is good. In the creation narrative in Genesis (1:1—2:4) we see God calling the world out of nothingness. The work is planned and careful, and God is pleased with it. No fewer than seven times in that first chapter do we read that God looked on what he had created and saw that it was good: light, water and dry land, vegetation, the sun and the moon, fish and birds and cattle and reptiles, human beings. In God's eyes, it's all good—very good.

Whatever else may have happened since then, whatever we short-sighted human beings may have done to God's skilled handiwork, the world started out as good, and not even we are bad enough to ruin the goodness that God laid down at its foundation.

There has been much speculation over the centuries about *how* God created the world. People used to think that each species of animal and plant was specifically and individually created by God. Now we are more inclined to think that God created a process, a process that may have started eight or ten billion years ago and has been unfolding ever since. Whatever we may think about such matters, it is clear that the Book of Genesis is not intended to be a scientific treatise about *how* the world was created. It is rather a religious book about *who* and *what*. It is God who is the source of the world, and what God created was and is good.

Genesis is also about *why*. God created the world for the same reason that human beings write poetry and sing songs: He wanted to express himself. Given the right circumstances, each of us likes to say who and what we are, to speak our heart. It's the same with God. God expresses himself in this world of ours, and what God expresses is goodness. God created the world because God is good and wanted others to share in that goodness. And wanting to share goodness is another name for love.

God created the world out of love because he wanted to express his goodness and share it with stars and planets, with palm trees and morning glory vines, with cows and pigs, and, yes, even with us.

One of the prominent non-believing scientists of our time has said that we are such insignificant creatures on a minor planet of an average star at the outer suburbs of a hundred thousand million galaxies that it's difficult to believe in a God who would care about us or even notice our existence. In my opinion, that's faulty logic. The fact that creation is bigger than we once thought doesn't mean that God is any less involved in it. It simply means that our idea of God has probably been too limited. It's not at all difficult to believe that God notices our existence or cares about us, no matter how big his creation may be, if God is our loving Creator. We are always insignificant and unimportant in comparison with God, but God doesn't love us because of our significance or importance. God loves us because God is God.

Of course, there is pain and suffering in the world, and we'll be saying something more about that later. Some of it comes of our own doing and that of human beings who have lived before us. Some of it seems meaningless and cruel. But even that doesn't mean that God is cruel or that creation is inherently flawed. It means that God's love for creation is so great that he is able to express and bring about goodness even when we can't understand how.

We live in a great and good and wonderful creation. We're just beginning to find out how vast it is, and we haven't come close to learning about or appreciating the little corner of it that God has given to us to enjoy. And it all runs on God's love.

Thinking Catholic involves a hardheaded, objective and loving appreciation of God's work of creation. The world is not an accident, not a dungeon, not just a vale of tears (even though we sometimes have done our best to make it that). The world is God's doing, created with a purpose, and that purpose is to let others share in divine goodness and love.

At the same time, thinking Catholic does not mean overlooking the real suffering and evil in the world. These things are there and we are called to do something about them. But suffering and evil are only the ground clutter on the weather map of God's work. God sees the world today as God saw it at the end of that first work of creation. It was very good then and it is very good now.

That's why thinking Catholic involves radical optimism. It's not inappropriate to be concerned about war, poverty and disease. It's not bad to be distressed about drug abuse, divorce and rampant selfishness. Thinking Catholic does not mean denying that we live in a crazy world. But however crazy the world may be, it is still God's world, it is still a good world and, no matter what else happens, God's love still makes the world go round.

If we are going to keep ourselves attuned to the fundamental reality and meaning of God's world, it's important to exercise regular and conscious appreciation of it, to acknowledge the beauty of the sunset, the freshness of a summer breeze, the wonder of dinosaur bones buried in a desert, the mind-boggling multiplicity of the stars, the seemingly infinite variety of earthly plants and animals. (I have subscribed to *National Geographic* for a long time. I find it helps me be attentive to the magnificence of God's world.)

We also need to reflect on and be grateful for the gifts that God has put into human minds and hearts: gifts of expression in words and stone and paint and music, gifts of thought and insight, gifts of self-sacrifice and affection. God's wisdom, goodness and love are imprinted all over this world of ours. The wise and faithful person is the one who knows how to recognize them and rejoice in them.

How we look on the world determines how we see everything else. Thinking Catholic involves recognizing the world as the canticle of God's goodness and love and being willing to sing along.

For Discussion and Reflection
• *What aspects of creation convince you that the world is good?*
• *Do you find the world mostly comfortable or mostly frightening? Why?*
• *Do you find it easy to be optimistic? Why? Why not?*

CHAPTER TWO

GUESTS AT GOD'S CELEBRATION

The world that God created does not belong to us. It belongs to God. We are guests here, invited for a temporary stay while permanent arrangements are being made for us. But while we are here, God has plans for us.

To begin with, God wants us to enjoy what he has created. God wants us to have a good time at this celebration of his goodness and love. The vastness, variety and beauty of what God has created are intended to give pleasure not just to him, but to us as well. God doesn't mean for us to be wallflowers at the celebration, waiting quietly until it's time to go home. God means for us to be part of what's going on. He wants us to relish the sights and sounds that he has put here for us. God wants us to mingle with the other guests and to derive pleasure from their company. It's OK to laugh, talk and sing along with the music. It's OK to applaud. It's OK to "ooh" and "aah" at the gifts that God gives his guests. It's OK to encourage others to enjoy them with us. To do otherwise would be to imply that God didn't do a very good job in expressing himself in creation. Enchantment with the wonder of God's creation is one of the qualities that make people like Saint Francis of Assisi so attractive.

Of course, we have to enjoy the celebration appropriately. It's God's party, not ours. We are guests in somebody else's home. We are not free to take over what God has provided for us and turn it to purposes that God didn't intend. Unfortunately, we seem to be pretty good at doing just that. Right from the beginning, the first human participants in the celebration tried to take it over and push God out of the way. They wanted to be hosts rather than guests, masters of the household rather than visitors.

People have been doing the same thing ever since. We take God's gift of speech, for example, and use it to hurt others. We take the strength and ingenuity that God has given us and use it to make wars or to impose injustice on others. Sometimes it seems as if the whole party has gotten out of hand and we are involved in a pagan orgy rather than a godly celebration.

At one point, the world got so bad that God sent his own Son to get things back on track. Jesus came to announce the coming of the kingdom of God, a state in which everything is under God's loving control once more and the party restored to sanity. One of the images that Jesus liked to use to describe the kingdom was a banquet, an ordered gathering in which everybody is having a good time. The kingdom began with Jesus and is still with us. The celebration and the sharing of God's goodness and love haven't ended. It's still going on despite the misbehavior of the guests. Creation is still good and God still intends us to enjoy it.

But there's more. God doesn't mean for us just to be grateful spectators or passive recipients in the celebration. He wants us to contribute to it. One of the most important gifts that God has given us is the gift of sharing in his creativity.

God has enabled us to take the raw materials of creation and turn them into medicines and statues and automobiles and houses and computers. God has given us the capacity to discover the complexity and beauty of creation and to share our discoveries with others in words and pictures and music. God has gifted us with the ability to learn how to grow crops and raise animals and even make whole new varieties of living things for our well-being and enjoyment. What God saw as good in the beginning was only the beginning. Much more has happened since then because of God's invitation to us to participate in the creative celebration.

Most important of all, God has invited and enabled us to participate in the creation of ourselves. We begin as helpless infants, dependent on others for everything. But as time goes by, we begin to make decisions and choices for ourselves. Those decisions and choices, based on the potential that God has given to each of us, gradually determine what we become. The helpless infant becomes a rocket scientist or a farmer or a doctor or a concert violinist or a priest. The dependent baby grows up to become a parent, passing on and shaping the gift of life in new human beings.

We can use the potential that God has given us to turn into thoughtful and generous human beings. We can be men and women who are grateful and attentive to God, consciously aware of the goodness and love around us. It all depends on how we use the capacities that God has given us to participate in the celebration.

That's not to say it's easy. Making good choices can be very demanding, thanks to our limited perspective and the selfishness that comes with our fallen human nature. We create ourselves a little bit at a time. Becoming a good human being takes at least as much effort and practice as becoming an Olympic athlete.

Sometimes we are inclined to give up and just drift along. But when we do that, we are letting circumstances or other people make our decisions for us. To refuse to expend the effort to make ourselves something beautiful for God is to opt out of our part in the celebration.

In June 1996 in Cincinnati, we observed the one hundred and seventy-fifth anniversary of the foundation of our diocese with a solemn liturgy of thanksgiving. The clergy, religious and laypeople of the archdiocese were invited as well as others who had been connected with our local church over the years. There were all kinds of committees to look after the invitations, the comfort of the guests from outside the diocese, the planning of the anniversary liturgy, the music and the reception outside the cathedral afterward. Lots of people worked very hard to bring the event to a successful outcome. It was a wonderful celebration and it was no less a celebration because of the planning and effort that it required. In fact, those who had helped bring the celebration about experienced a level of satisfaction beyond that of the guests.

Our contribution to God's celebration of goodness and love does indeed require persistence, patience and effort. But it's still celebration.

Thinking Catholic involves conscious participation in God's celebration. We are not in a prison in which we wait for our sentence to be ended so that we can leave. We are at a party, and God means for us to have a good time and help others have a good time, too.

Of course, our life on this earth is not a period of mindless hilarity. Life is serious business, and God wants us to take it seriously. But the seriousness is not the seriousness of enduring a punishment. It's the effort required to make our contribution to the celebration. Life is not a burden to be borne but a gift to be appreciated and responded to.

Those who think Catholic know that it is good to be alive. They take pleasure in the gifts that God has provided for them. They are grateful. They are also attentive to the capabilities that God has given them to make the celebration even better. They are not content just to listen to the music. They are also anxious to perform as skillfully as they can the particular part that God has assigned to them.

For Discussion and Reflection
- *How do you celebrate the goodness of creation?*
- *What decisions of yours have made you what you are?*
- *Are you having a good time at God's party?*

CHAPTER THREE

OUR HOST IS WITH US

It would be a strange host who gave a party and didn't show up personally or who appeared at the beginning to get things started and then disappeared. We expect our host to be around during a celebration, not only to see that the guests are well attended to, but also to take part in the party.

God is a good host. God didn't set up the celebration of his goodness and love and then walk away, intending to return at the end to turn off the lights and clean up the mess. No, God is part of the celebration, present and active at every phase. Thinking Catholic involves being aware of our host and being able to recognize him, not only to reassure ourselves that he is still around, but also to learn from him what is going on and how we are expected to respond.

There are many ways to see God in creation. Everything that *is* is somehow created to reflect God. We can see the power of God in the thunderstorm and the immensity of God in the sky and the sea. A cat licking her kittens shows us something about God's tenderness. The seemingly limitless variety of plants is an indication of the generosity of God who was not content to create just a few species, but thousands and thousands for our use and enjoyment. When we enter the realm of the human, the images of God are even more varied. Tall people and short people, creative people and plodding people, people with gifts of affectivity and people with gifts of logic and mental discipline, people who talk and laugh a lot and people who are quiet and reserved—all of them reflect something about God.

Of course, the imprint of God isn't always obvious—it's hard to see God in a cockroach. But God's imprint is there somewhere. For that matter, finding God in a rose or a sunset is not inevitable unless we are willing to look for him there. God's imprint in creation is like one of those puzzles in the Sunday paper that appears to be a meaningless jumble of colors and lines until we look at it in a certain way and come to recognize the picture that is there. Part of thinking Catholic is knowing how to look at the picture.

But God's presence at the celebration is not limited to imprints and images left behind for us to look at. God is also personally present and active in what's going on here.

For one thing, God's power, and therefore God's presence, is active just in keeping things going. If God were to withdraw his love and attention from creation for even a moment, all the countless galaxies with their stars and planets (including little Earth off in the outer suburbs) would simply lapse back into nothingness. The simple fact that things *are* indicates that God is around somewhere. If he weren't, there would be nothing.

But that's not all. If God has enabled and invited us human beings to participate in and contribute to the celebration, and if we can only be and act through the power and the presence of the Creator, then our interaction with one another is also a manifestation of the presence of God. A mother's care for her child, a husband's concern for his wife, the affection of friends for one another, a priest's dedication to his people—all are ultimately actions of God who is there, who is in them all.

Sometimes it's hard to see the presence and action of God in what people do to one another. Is God active in the child abuser and the war criminal? Yes, at least insofar as he has given these people life and some basic human capabilities. The difficulty in seeing God arises from the misuse and distortion of God's presence in these persons. The challenge is to be willing to look behind the evil and see that even this terrible behavior cannot totally obliterate the godliness that lies deep inside them.

But the presence of God goes beyond anonymous action in maintaining the world and in enabling human beings to do good for one another. God is also in touch with us directly and in his own name.

We Christians believe that God speaks to us in the Bible. These narratives of kings and prophets and miracles, these collections of wise sayings, these letters and visions from long ago are God's word to us. God is in them as much as we are in the words we speak to one another. Their meaning for us here and now is not always obvious. God has not chosen to address us in words and images that even a child can understand. This may be because the truth God wants to communicate to us is more complex than that, or because he wants us to have to exert some effort to grasp the meaning so that we will understand it better. Yet the fact remains that the Lord is present in his word.

The Lord is also present in the community of believers that we call church. The Risen Jesus promised to be with this community forever, to love its members through their love for one another, to protect them in time of trial. Catholics look on the church as the Body of Christ, a body whose soul is the Holy Spirit, a body whose activity is the ongoing activity of Christ.

In the context of the church, God is most intensely present in the sacraments. Every time one of the sacraments is celebrated, God the Father acts in Christ his Son through the Holy Spirit: to begin his life in us, or to forgive our sins, or strengthen us in times of illness, or make us extensions of his love in marriage or ordained ministry. The capstone of the sacraments, of course, is the Holy Eucharist in which Christ himself, personally and really, comes to nourish our life in him and to make his presence accessible to us as friend and brother.

The master of the celebration is indeed with us. In fact, like a good host, God is all over the place, in countless ways, in countless manifestations. Yet he is a polite host who doesn't impose himself on his guests at every moment, who doesn't intrude on what they may be engaged in. He waits to be recognized.

Thinking Catholic means being able to recognize and appreciate the presence of God in our lives. This is something a little different from knowing about God or acknowledging God's authority and power. It involves consciously being with God.

This requires practice. We have to form the habit of looking for God, of searching out his presence in nature, in other people and in our own hearts. We have to keep calling ourselves to attentiveness to him even when we listen to Sacred Scripture or participate in the celebration of the sacraments.

We human beings sometimes seem to suffer from a sort of natural nearsightedness and superficiality, probably due to our inherited inclination to sin. We are fascinated with the immediate and the obvious, with our own personal needs and wants. It takes a little effort to accustom ourselves to look beyond all that.

When I was in the seminary and it was prayer time, the prayer leader would always say, "Let us put ourselves into the presence of God." It was an invitation to refocus, to leave some of our baggage behind, to close off the noise, to look toward different horizons and to open ourselves to the Lord. Yet we don't have to be at formal, organized prayer in order to put ourselves into the presence of God. We can accustom ourselves to doing it in just about every aspect of our life: when we get up in the morning, as we start our work, when we begin our meals, when we meet a friend, even when we are just walking down the street. We can always put ourselves into the presence of God because God is always present in one way or another.

Thinking Catholic means living our life in awareness of the company of our host.

For Discussion and Reflection

• *Where do you see God in your life?*

• *Where do you find it hardest to see God in the world?*

• *In what ways do you try to be aware of the presence of God?*

CHAPTER FOUR

LIFE ON LOAN

People who don't know much at all about Catholic thinking do know that Catholics are against abortion and assisted suicide. If they are a little better informed, they know that Catholic teaching is also opposed to artificial contraception and test-tube babies. Since these things are more or less accepted in our society, the general public sometimes looks on the Catholic position on these matters as old-fashioned, at best quaint and at worst socially divisive. Why don't Catholics get with it and join the modern world? Why don't they change their rules and stop making trouble for society at large?

The Catholic position on these matters is not a set of laws laid down by church leaders. It is a direct consequence of thinking Catholic about the most fundamental elements of human existence.

Creation is the expression of God's goodness and love, a celebration in which human beings are called to share and an ongoing process to which human beings are called to contribute. It's God's show, not ours, and individual human life is not a possession that we have been given to use as we see fit, but an instrument that God loans us to enable us to carry out our part in his plans.

Moreover, of all the gifts that God has entrusted to us our life is the most basic, because life is the fundamental condition of the process of human existence. It's not just one faculty among many, like speech or thought. Human life is the vehicle for everything else, the operating system on which all God's programs run.

All human life belongs to God—my life and the life of every other human being past, present and future. And all human life is given for God's purposes. This is the fundamental insight that distinguishes Catholic thinking from much of the craziness of the rest of the world.

If human life is given to us on loan to use for God's purposes, then it is not right for me to end my human life when I see fit. To do so is to opt out of the celebration, to indicate that I want no further part in what is going on in creation, that I want to leave the party before my part in it is completed.

Likewise, if each human life is a unique gift from God, it is not right for me to take the life of another human being, whether it is the life of a personal enemy or a convicted criminal, of a sick friend or an unborn child. It's not up to us to interfere in the plans that God may have for other people.

Again, if human life is given as a gift of God and for God's purposes, it is not right to do as we please with the processes by which human life comes into being. To try to bring human beings into existence exclusively in accord with our wishes and our convenience, to try to have children born according to our particular specifications constitutes interference with one of the most basic acts of the Creator.

When we tamper with human life in these ways, we are not only abusing our privileges as guests at God's celebration. We are also, in effect, trying to take over the celebration by controlling the guest list. It is a particularly extreme attempt to oust the host and put ourselves in his place.

This is all part of thinking Catholic. Much of the world around us would say that if Catholics want to think that way, they are free to do so as long as they allow other people to do as they see fit in these matters. But it's not that simple.

Abusing human life is not just a matter of acting in disaccord with a given religious mindset. It also brings natural and inevitable consequences of its own. You can't interfere with the way things are made to be and not expect something else to go wrong.

When people decide, as many in our crazy world have decided, that human life is a personal possession, ours to do with as we see fit, they open the door to all sorts of unexpected horrors. If suicide is acceptable, then why should I ever endure hardships, pain and struggle of any sort? Why not just end it all today? If it is acceptable to help a sick relative commit suicide when that person's life is too burdensome to him or her, what is wrong with persuading that person to commit suicide when his or her life is too burdensome to me?

If it is acceptable to terminate the life of an unborn child when that life seems to threaten its mother, why can it be wrong to end the unborn life that is merely inconvenient? For that matter, what's wrong with ending the life of a child already born if the child is more than the parents think they can handle? (We have already reached the point in our society where it is legally acceptable to kill a partially born child.) Once people have accepted the idea of custom-made children, conceived according to the timetable and the description specified by the parents—or parent—how is the child different from other objects that we can order up according to our individual desires?

Human experience in these last few decades, both here in the United States and elsewhere, seems to be teaching us that treating human life as a possession creates more problems than it is intended to solve. Some thinking people, even those who do not think Catholic, are beginning to see that human society can survive only if human life is held inviolable, universally protected by government and beyond the reach of private individuals. Human beings are simply not equipped to be in arbitrary control of human life.

Of course people don't interfere with human life—their own or that of others—because they want to destroy human society. They do so because human life can be painful, frustrating and difficult.

From the perspective of public policy, the response to these realities ought to be that, in spite of pain, frustration and difficulty, it is still better in the long run to keep our hands off human life because of the terrible things that seem to happen when we begin to interfere with it. We simply don't know enough to be in charge.

Thinking Catholic provides a more reassuring perspective. We don't deny the pain and effort that is part of every human life. But we are also aware that God's view and ours are sometimes different. We tend to be shortsighted and think that there is something wrong with a life that is not pleasant or productive here and now. God doesn't look only at the here and now. God looks at the life of each of us in the light of the contribution that it makes to the plan of creation, the plan of goodness and love in which we participate. We don't have to understand everything. We can't, any more than children can understand why they have to go to the dentist. God is good enough and wise enough to bring benefit to his creation and blessing to us even out of terminal cancer and deformed children and total human failure.

Thinking Catholic includes the conviction that God knows what he is doing in each of us, that he uses the basic instrument that he has loaned to us, our individual human life, for purposes that surpass our immediate awareness. It's not for us to destroy or tamper with the instrument because we happen not to understand what God is doing with it. Unqualified respect for the gift of life is an essential component of thinking Catholic.

For Discussion and Reflection

• *How do you express respect for human life?*
• *Have you ever found human life—your own or someone else's—to be burdensome?*
• *How do you react to people whose lives seem unproductive?*

CHAPTER FIVE

A HAPPY ENDING

Sometimes it's hard to believe that this world we share is really God's world, and still harder to believe that it is a celebration of goodness and love. Sin, pain, frustration and evil are everywhere.

We are all personally acquainted with sickness and struggle. Disappointment is part of everybody's life. Sometimes it seems that, no matter how hard we try, things just don't turn out right. Inside each of us are inclinations toward selfishness and sin which, in our better moments, we know are invitations to greater or lesser degrees of self-destruction. Acquiring bad habits is easy, and rooting them out is hard. Whole schools of philosophy have looked on these realities and concluded that our individual human life is an exercise in frustration, meaninglessness or boredom.

Things are not much better when we look on human history as a whole. We have come a long way from the Stone Age to the computer age. We presently enjoy comforts and capabilities that were beyond our great-grandparents' imagination. Yet in other ways, we are worse off than we were before. Values of family life that most people once took for granted are disappearing. It seems that the education of our young people has degenerated into damage control. New sicknesses have arisen that we are unable to control. Economic betterment for some is too often connected with impoverishment for others. We have still not found ways to resolve human conflicts. The wars of the past seem almost humane compared with the armed struggles of our own lifetime and with the destructive capabilities that we have prepared for the future. We have now reached a point where we are likely to destroy the world itself if we are not careful, and we don't have a very good track record in guarding against destruction.

In view of all that, this world and this life may not seem like much of a celebration, but more like a catastrophe, an exercise in pointlessness or, at best, a good plan that has gone awry and whose ending can only be destruction when God has finally grown tired of it.

Thinking Catholic helps us see things differently. There is no denying the reality of evil. It is real. It is destructive. But those who think Catholic know that human selfishness, blindness and destructiveness are not going to be the last word. We live in hope, in the conviction that better things lie ahead and that God is good enough, wise enough and powerful enough to bring his good plans to fulfillment in spite of all the ingenuity and willfulness of the human heart.

If God had intended to write off creation, he has had every chance to do so over the millennia of human history. But that's not what God did. Instead he sent his Son to start over, to institute a new creation that lives in Christ and that will live and grow as long as Christ is with us—and he promised to be with us forever. This new creation will conclude when Christ comes in glory to take all that is good in creation to himself in the final stage of the kingdom of God.

Jesus is everything that God ever intended humanity to be. And what Jesus came to be and to do will determine the final form and the final fulfillment of creation. It will all somehow be like him when he gathers it to himself in the kingdom.

Jesus made it quite clear that we don't need to understand how that's going to come about, still less when it's going to happen. But he has promised that it will be so. Thinking Catholic means taking him at his word.

But the final saving of creation, its victory over all the viciousness of human self-will, is not something that Christ Jesus is going to bring about all alone. The drama of God's love doesn't have just one hero, but a whole cast of them. Jesus invites each of us to be in that cast.

In the shorthand terminology of thinking Catholic, we speak of heaven and hell. Good people end up in heaven for all eternity, bad people in hell. Sometimes we oversimplify and find ourselves thinking about heaven and hell as places, and about the process of getting there as a kind of bookkeeping operation in which God totals up the accounts of good and evil in the life of each of us and comes up with a closing balance that determines where we go.

There's some truth in that, but the reality is a little more complex. God doesn't just give us a series of tests to pass in order to squeak into heaven. Rather, God invites us to work with him in the salvation of creation. God gives us a share in the life of Christ when we are baptized, and we spend the rest of our life responding to that gift.

If we are faithful to our calling to continue the life and mission of Christ, we gradually grow more and more into the kingdom. We are more and more conscious of the goodness and love of God. We are more and more eager to share that goodness and love with the people around us, sometimes in big ways, sometimes in little ways, sometimes at the cost of great sacrifice, sometimes through acts of kindness and consideration that are almost automatic. Through our life Christ's kingdom grows a little stronger in the world and we ourselves grow more and more at home in the presence of the Lord, more and more at one with God's ways of seeing and doing. When our earthly life reaches its conclusion, we continue living, only now it is in the fully revealed presence of God. We "go to heaven," not because of some final decision on God's part, but because of what we have become in our years of earthly collaboration with God's celebration of goodness and love. God doesn't merely decide to let us in. It's where we belong.

Those who reject God's offer to collaborate in his plans drift further and further away from the purpose of creation. They center themselves on secondary or destructive things, sometimes through consciously made big decisions, sometimes through a series of smaller, less conscious ones that gradually eat away at their connection with God until they themselves determine that participating in God's plans is no longer important. Instead of working to bring the kingdom of Christ closer in themselves and in others, they impede its growth.

Finally, when there are no more choices to be made, they find that all that is left is the kingdom of heaven or eternal detachment from it. Since they have spent their lives walking away from the kingdom, all that is left for them is to be a failure forever, an eternal outsider. God has not created hell as a place where he can put bad people. People create hell for themselves and put themselves in it by their rejection and destruction of what God had in mind for them.

Thinking Catholic doesn't mean trying to believe that sick people are not sick, that human suffering is merely an illusion, or that human sinfulness is of no consequence. Thinking Catholic does not mean trying to convince ourselves that everything is really all right here and now. Not everything is all right here and now, and there is no point in pretending otherwise. But thinking Catholic does involve the conviction that somehow, sometime things will be all right, even if we can't understand how. Thinking Catholic involves the awareness of the power of the continuing life of Christ and of God's invitation to us to share that life forever.

Thinking Catholic means being realistic enough to look forward to a happy ending.

For Discussion and Reflection
• *Where do you see evil in the world?*
• *How do you participate in God's plans for the world?*
• *Do you expect to go to heaven?*

CHAPTER SIX

IT ALL DEPENDS

Maturity involves a sense of proportion. I suspect that most of us have had the experience of feeling that the world was going to come to an end because of something we did or something that happened to us. We did badly on an exam at school, we said something that we immediately knew was a terrible gaffe, we got sick and couldn't go to the party we had been looking forward to, we had a flat tire on the way to a job interview.

Our first reaction was to think that life was over for us, that the world held no further joy, that we would be better off dead. Then time passed and the world went on in spite of what had happened. Soon we picked up where we left off and found that there was still life ahead of us.

In retrospect, we may now even be able to discover some good that came of what at first seemed like catastrophe. We begin to see the thing in a different perspective. We grow up a little bit and our sense of proportion deepens. That terrible thing was relative to our stage of personal development and to the circumstances of the moment.

Thinking Catholic, which is another name for Christian maturity, involves an awareness of how much in our life is relative: relative to our capacity to understand and endure it, relative to our state of mind, relative to the goals and values that guide our lives. Our life doesn't become worthless or meaningless because of anything that happens to us or even because of anything we do to ourselves. It all depends on what we make of it, on the way it fits in with God's enduring love and care for us.

What's important in our lives is not so much *what* happens as *how we deal* with the events: the direction in which we choose to orient them, the value and the meaning that we find in them. This is true whether what happens is something that seems good or bad.

Most people would be glad to be so wealthy that they never have to worry about money again. There's nothing wrong with that, but the real significance of wealth for a person's life depends on what the person does with these resources. Using wealth to ride roughshod over others, to demand attention, to set oneself up in mindless comfort and needless consumption is one thing. Using wealth as a means to help others and make God's goodness more immediate for them is something else.

The greatest human achievements can be turned into self-indulgence and even misery if they are not properly oriented, while "ordinary" human success, like holding down a decent job and raising a family, can bring a degree of happiness that more conspicuously "successful" people might never enjoy. It all depends.

It's the same with trials and sufferings. Some people emerge from suffering with a deepened sense of the meaning of their lives, with gratitude and appreciation for what they have experienced. Others emerge broken and embittered. What matters is what you do with it.

Developing an appropriate understanding of what happens in our lives is difficult for us human beings because we tend to be so childish and so nearsighted. If it feels good, we just want to sit back and enjoy it without bothering to find out what else is involved and what responsibilities may be associated with it. If it feels bad, we want to fix it immediately so that the hurt will go away, regardless of what else may be involved. We tend to absolutize both pleasure and pain, whereas both depend for their meaning on other, far more important matters.

Whether we feel good or bad is not of primary importance. Whether we are a success or a failure as the world counts success and failure is not what matters. What really matters is how our lives fit into our role in God's plan of goodness and love. Everything else depends on that.

In this context, we might do well to reflect on the life and death of Jesus. By any merely human standards, Jesus' life was a failure. He didn't get much recognition from important people. The men and women who did follow him were not prominent or powerful. Some of his followers were significantly unimpressive. In the end he was scorned, derided and put to death by one of the most painful methods that human ingenuity has been able to devise. From one perspective, all this was an insignificant episode in ancient history. From another, this was the most significant human life that has ever been lived. It was the one human existence that fully satisfied God's expectations from human beings. It was the human life that restored God's order in creation and that offered a new worth and meaning to all those who would accept a share in it. It wasn't just what happened to Jesus that gave meaning to his life. It was how he dealt with what happened that was important, the meaning it acquired from his dedication to the love of the heavenly Father.

Thinking Catholic means looking on the events of our human existence with the proper perspective. Not much that happens to us is of irreversible importance. For the person who thinks Catholic, life is too short and too involved with more significant matters to spend much attention on things that other people may find important.

That's why laughter is a prominent dimension of thinking Catholic. Laughter is the human response to the incongruous, the unexpected and the disproportionate. We laugh when we are able to see the little side of supposedly big things. People who think Catholic are likely to laugh a lot.

This is not to say that thinking Catholic involves an ongoing state of mindless merriment, of laughing off everything. No, the kind of spiritual maturity that is expressed in thinking Catholic does see importance in the happenings of our life. Human successes and human hurts are not simply insignificant. Those who think Catholic have to come to grips with suffering and failure. But they see these things as temporary and as part of a whole. These things are not the last word, the final determinant of the worth and direction of our lives. They are merely episodes in the drama that constitutes a human existence, sometimes tragic episodes, sometimes episodes of comic relief. Even if the significance of the episode is not immediately clear, those who think Catholic know that the drama as a whole is going to have a happy ending. Everything has to be seen in relationship to that ending.

Jesus tells his disciples that if they seek first the kingdom of God, everything else will fall into place (see Matthew 6:33). He doesn't say that everything else is meaningless, but secondary, relative to the principal action. Seeking the kingdom means being open to the goodness and love that God offers us in Christ as the fundamental element of our life. Nothing else is equally important. Everything else derives its importance from its relationship to God's love and care for us.

Thinking Catholic means seeing the significance of what is really significant and seeing the relative insignificance of everything else. It all depends on that.

For Discussion and Reflection

• *What failures have you experienced?*
• *What successes have you enjoyed?*
• *What makes you laugh?*

CHAPTER SEVEN

SINNERS ALL

Every Catholic knows the Hail Mary. It's a prayer we say frequently, and every time we pray it we remind ourselves of what we are: "Holy Mary, mother of God, pray for us sinners...." We are sinners, each and every one of us.

Sin plays a significant part in thinking Catholic. We know that we are born into original sin. We are not associated with God at the beginning of our lives as our first parents were at the beginning of creation. Something is missing in us that they had, something they lost when they tried to take over God's role as host in the celebration. In addition, there is the sinfulness in the world around us, sinfulness so easy for us to learn to imitate. Then there are our own sins, big ones and small ones, the bad things we have done and the good things we have deliberately left undone. Each of us in his or her own way, to a greater or lesser extent, has played Adam and Eve in our relationship with our heavenly Father. Being aware of sinfulness is part of being Catholic. We know that what the author of the First Letter of John told the early Christians also applies to us: "If we say, 'We are without sin,' we deceive ourselves, and the truth is not in us" (1 John 1:8).

There is a whole branch of theology concerned (at least in part) with sin: moral theology. Catholic moral theologians over the centuries have studied sin, classified it and evaluated its various manifestations. They have analyzed the conditions that lead to sin and the various requirements of understanding and will that contribute to the gravity of sins. There isn't much about sin that hasn't been studied by Catholic thinking.

Given all this, it might seem that thinking Catholic demands an ongoing state of conscious guilt, a consistent awareness of failure and incompleteness. But that's only one aspect of thinking Catholic about sin. The Catholic mindset also includes an awareness of God's desire to pardon, to forgive, to express his ongoing love and care for us in spite of our real and serious deficiencies.

That's why Catholic thinking about sin always includes the sacrament of reconciliation, that unique encounter of God, the church and the sinner in which the individual expresses his or her guilt and, through the agency of the church, receives forgiveness from God. Sin is an integral part of thinking Catholic, but so is God's mercy and love. You can never have one without the other if you are really thinking Catholic.

There are other ways to approach human sinfulness. One is to say there is no such thing. The idea that certain kinds of human behavior are inherently wrong and necessarily harmful to those who engage in them is outmoded. We may need human laws to keep antisocial behavior under control, but as long as what we do doesn't harm other people, we don't need to be concerned about it. The idea of sin is an attempt to keep people from doing what comes naturally to them. This approach to sin is quite common in the crazy world around us.

Another approach is to see our sinfulness as so deeply rooted and so much a part of our lives that there really isn't anything we can do about it. We can only acknowledge ourselves as totally powerless from the beginning and hope that God won't be as hard on us as we deserve when our life is over.

Both approaches are kinds of denial. The first denies that sin is real and is harmful and destructive to the sinner, apart from what it might do to other people. The second denies that God has any interest in what we do here and now. God simply allows us to go on sinning until the end, when, without any collaboration on our part, he either cleans up the mess we have made or writes us off completely.

Thinking Catholic denies nothing. It is quite clear about our sinfulness. Sin is real. It is common. It is ours. Each of us is born in detachment from God, and, even after God has united us with himself and his plans in Christ, we keep wanting to go off in other directions. None of us is particularly successful in playing the part that God has assigned to us in his celebration of goodness and love. We are too affected by the evil around us, too scarred by the wrong decisions we have made, too weakened by our own self-destructive acts and omissions. There's no way to deny that and still be in touch with sane reality.

But thinking Catholic is also realistic about God's response to our sinfulness. God never gives up on us. God loves us in spite of what we have done or not done. God still wants us to participate in the celebration of creation. All he asks is that we acknowledge our sinfulness and accept once more his love for us. It's not that what we have done is not wrong or not destructive of God's handiwork in us. But God's love for us is greater than the greatest wrong we can inflict on ourselves or on God's good creation. We are all flawed merchandise, but God remains willing to have us anyhow.

Thinking Catholic about sin has a lot to be said for it. It teaches us that we don't have to pretend that we are not really sinners, that what we have done, in spite of the accusations of our heart, is not really bad, that everything is really all right, or somebody else's fault, or the result of forces within us that we simply can't control. Thinking Catholic about sin allows us to look ourselves directly in the eye and tell the truth about ourselves: We are sinners all. The best of us is infected by failure, and there is no way out of our plight except the free and ever-present love and mercy of God.

Thinking Catholic about sin also assures us that we don't have to achieve. God doesn't sit back to see what we are going to make of things and then, on the basis of what we have done with ourselves, determine whether or not we are worth anything. God knows from the beginning that none of us is worth much if left on our own, so he stands by us every step of the way, even when we are going off in the wrong direction. At the end, if we are still open to him in any way, he welcomes us into the kingdom. What God welcomes is not the wonderful production that we have made of ourselves, but the result of the workings of his love on admittedly unpromising material.

If we are thinking Catholic, we know that even our sinfulness is relative. It is not the last word unless we choose to make it so. It is not for that reason any less bad, destructive, rebellious, prevalent or real. It is simply not the whole picture. The whole picture has to include the love of the Creator for this self-seeking creature who finds it so hard to act responsibly. It has to include God's unlimited forgiveness and mercy for this so frequently unsuccessful production of his.

Thinking Catholic involves reassurance that God loves us in spite of our sins and confidence that, even though our life is not an unqualified success, it is still precious to God.

Thinking Catholic enables us to stand before the Lord with a smile of expectation, even as we acknowledge that we are sinners all.

For Discussion and Reflection

• *How do you deal with sin in your life?*
• *How have you experienced God's mercy?*
• *What have you learned from your sins?*

CHAPTER EIGHT

SIGNIFICANT OTHERS

Thinking Catholic is not done in the first person singular. It always involves the plural. It's not concerned with *me* but with *us*. While each of us is a unique individual, custom-made by the Creator and loved by God as the special persons we are, we never stand alone either in the sight of God or in the execution of our role in the celebration that is creation. Significant others are always included.

We all need other people to survive. We human beings are totally helpless when we are born. We need years of care before we can begin to think of existing without the hour-by-hour attention of our parents. And the care we need is not just physical. We have to be trained to walk and to speak, to act and to think. The values that motivate us and the goals we will pursue in our lives come to us almost exclusively from our family, at least until we reach a certain level of maturity. We simply cannot do without others.

That's why the family plays such a big part in thinking Catholic. Catholics are opposed to divorce and remarriage and to casual sexual activity not because Catholics are old-fashioned, but because they have an acute awareness of just how important the family is to the well-being of its members. How can children grow up to know about unconditional love and self-sacrifice if they grow up with confusing or destructive experiences of parenthood and family life? Our families make us what we are and, in spite of what our world seems to think, it is not likely that a truly healthy human being will grow and flourish in an unhealthy family.

But the significance of others does not lie just in what we can do for each other. At a deeper level, the significance of others lies in what they are.

One of the most deeply held tenets of thinking Catholic is that each and every human being is valuable. Everybody is important. Everybody counts. From the rocket scientist to the seemingly hopeless alcoholic, from the pope to the war criminal, no human being can rightly be disregarded, written off, thrown away.

The reason we see worth in every human person is that each of us is part of God's creation, called to play his or her special part in the celebration of God's goodness and love. All human persons are precious to the Lord. If that were not so, they wouldn't be here. We may not be able to see or appreciate their worth, but that's not the issue. We are not in charge of the celebration, God is; and it is up to us to respect all the guests that God has invited to participate.

Given our dependence on others, given their own special value to God, it follows in thinking Catholic that we owe something to them. If we have been called to help God make the most of the celebration that constitutes creation, it is clear that the greatest share of our attention is owed to those others who have the most to contribute—God's human creatures. Because we share responsibility for creation, we share responsibility for one another.

We exercise this responsibility in many different ways. Parents exercise some of their responsibility through the love and care they give their children. Friends exercise responsibility in doing good for each other, in sharing burdens, in reflecting joys. We all contribute to the well-being of others by the work that we do, work that not only enables us to earn our living but also provides goods and services that make the lives of other people better. Even in the pocket change of daily life we recognize the significance of others by the kindness and courtesy with which we treat them. We may not even know who they are, but they are important.

We also express our responsibility for others in the pursuit of social justice. The poor, the unsuccessful, even the lazy and the criminal are not disposable items that we can throw into the garbage can of society if they prove to be without immediate usefulness. They are God's creatures, each as unique and precious to God as we are. To marginalize them, to compel them to live in misery, to refuse to take them into account as we mold our society is to overlook and mistreat what God has called both them and us to be. To be significant doesn't require that others attain a certain level of prosperity or success or usefulness. It requires only that they exist.

We are even called to love our enemies and do good to those who hate us. This command of the Lord is not just to challenge us or to spare us the self-destructiveness of hatred or to reduce conflict in the world. It's also to keep us aware that there is more to our enemy than his or her hostility to us and that that "more" has greater significance than the harm that we may experience at the enemy's hand.

It's easiest to extend ourselves for those we know best. We have received the most from them and our familiarity enables us to recognize the good that is in them. That's quite understandable. It's natural to love a neighbor. But we may not limit our concept of love of neighbor to response to the good that we receive or perceive.

One of the most memorable of Jesus' parables is the story of the Good Samaritan (Luke 10:29–37), whose point is that the relationship of neighbor does not depend on religious or national affinity, but on need. The fact that the other may be different or strange or unknown or even bad is irrelevant. Whoever can benefit from what I have to offer is my neighbor, and it is that person to whom I owe my attention.

Thinking Catholic includes the conviction that nobody is permitted to be a loner in this life, to limit himself or herself to taking what is wanted or needed and leaving everybody else to look after themselves. We have all received too much for that. Our responsibilities for creation are too broad for that. The others are too significant for that.

All this responsibility is not meant to constitute a burden, a never-ending task of attending to the needs of countless others. It is rather an opportunity to become conscious of the grand spectrum of human variety, to accustom ourselves to looking for the good in others rather than for their usefulness to us, to appreciate the gifts that each person has to offer to the celebration and to be grateful for the gifts that we have to offer to them.

Jean-Paul Sartre, one of the atheist philosophers of our time, has said that hell is other people. Thinking Catholic says that heaven is other people, that our happiness and theirs is determined to a great extent by what we have to offer to each other. The celebration will not be complete without the full participation of each guest. We are all significant to God. God looks on each of us with love and delight. Thinking Catholic means learning to look on other people with the eyes of God and to treasure them accordingly.

For Discussion and Reflection

- *How do you relate to your family?*
- *How do you exercise responsibility for others?*
- *What part has forgiveness played in your life?*

CHAPTER NINE

HAVING ISN'T HAPPINESS

The world in which we live runs on the presumption that the more people have, the more important they are and therefore the happier they are. The world pays the most attention to those who have most. Those who have lots of money and live in big houses and drive big cars are much more likely to have their words listened to and their wishes responded to than those who have less.

This crazy world keeps trying to persuade the rest of us that we, too, will be better off if we have more. That's why TV programs are written in ten- or twelve-minute segments: There will be more opportunities to sell things. The latest cars, the newest medications, the most stylish clothes, the best hammers and saws, the newest homes in the newest neighborhoods—insistently and persuasively we are told that we need these things, that we really can't get along without them, that having them will somehow make us happier. And once we have these things, we are told that's not really the end because now there are new and improved products that make the old ones obsolete. The implication in all of it is that our worth and our importance, and therefore our happiness, depend on what we have.

Obviously, we have to have some things. We can't get along without food and clothing. We need some sort of shelter. In our increasingly complex world, most people need their own means of transportation. If we want to stay in touch with what is going on around us, we need radios and television sets. In these last few years, it seems to have become necessary even for children to have a computer. We can't live with the same equipment that was sufficient for our grandparents.

There's nothing wrong with all that. God is pleased when we use the potential of his creation to improve our lives and make the best use of the capacities that he has put within us.

But possessions are also dangerous. For one thing, they can be addictive. Something inside us seems to keep clamoring for more. We find it difficult to limit our possessions to what we need. It seems that everything we get requires us to get something more. In its extreme form, this inclination leads to the compulsive spending that even the world recognizes as a mental disorder. In its more ordinary manifestation, this inclination to possess leads us to acquire things that we don't really need, just for the pleasure of having them, and, once we have them, to put them aside and go after something else. How many possessions do we have that we never really use or even enjoy? How many of our possessions could we throw away or give to somebody else without noticing the difference? To some extent we are all possession junkies, hooked on irrational getting and having.

But even more dangerous than the pursuit of possessions is the mentality that lies behind it. Our desire to have ever more is the expression of an inclination to make ourselves safe and independent, to surround ourselves with things so that we won't have to rely on anybody else, not even God, for our fulfillment. Implicit in the compulsion to have is the desire to set up our own little private celebration of life so that we won't have to bother with the celebration that God has invited us to. Apart from the radical discourtesy of such an attitude, it is also counterproductive. It won't bring us happiness, and it will deform our spirit.

The reason that possessions will not bring us happiness is that we are created for something else. God did not make us to latch onto things and to find our worth in what we have. God made us to participate in the ongoing celebration of creation, to make our particular contribution to the expression of his goodness and love, to want and to do good for those around us, to collaborate in his ongoing kindness and love. That's how we were meant to spend the years of our earthly existence, and only that can bring us fulfillment, only that can make us happy. If we direct ourselves to something less than that, if we try to find fulfillment in surrounding ourselves with secondary things like possessions, we are doomed to frustration. And, when the time comes to leave our possessions behind, we will find that our life has brought us only emptiness.

It's not just at the end that our possessions will betray us. They also deform us along the way. If we determine our value by what we have, we will soon find ourselves looking on other human beings as objects to be possessed rather than as significant others to be loved and respected. We will use people for our own purposes, and, once those purposes have been fulfilled, we will abandon them and look for others who can contribute in other ways to our personal enrichment. If things are the center of our lives, even human beings will become things for us.

But there's more. Our lives are governed and directed by the values and goals we espouse. What we want determines who and what we are. If we want lots of things, then those things govern and direct our earthly existence. Possessions are no longer instruments we use for a higher purpose; they become ends in themselves that take over our life. Instead of possessing our possessions, we will find that our possessions possess us.

Two manifestations of thinking Catholic call for special mention in this context of having and using. The first is vowed poverty. Within the community of the church are religious under vows who have promised the Lord that they will be as detached as possible from possessions. Their vow of poverty does not mean they live in misery or want, but that they own nothing for themselves and will use only that portion of the world's goods that is necessary for the work they do. Far from being depressed because of what they do not have, they generally find a great sense of freedom in their poverty. These vowed men and women religious may seem to the world to be marginally mad because of all the wonderful things they have given up. But to those who think Catholic they are a source of encouragement and a sign of sanity.

The other manifestation of thinking Catholic in this context goes by a name that we have recently begun to borrow from our Protestant brothers and sisters, although the kernel of it goes back to the teaching of Jesus. It is stewardship. Stewardship is a consciously developed awareness that what we possess we have on loan, that what we have been given has been given for God's work, that our own wants and needs have to be evaluated in the light of the needs of others, and that happiness does not consist in having a lot but in using wisely what we have. Stewardship is not some new gimmick that priests have thought up to increase Sunday contributions. It is, rather, a formula for sanity.

Thinking Catholic does not mean doing without possessions, but using what we have with care and gratitude to further God's purposes in creation. Those who think Catholic do enjoy the good things of the world, but they know that these things are only temporary and that they must be directed toward something beyond our individual satisfaction. Those who think Catholic use their possessions with detachment and with caution because they know how dangerous they can be. Above all, they know that happiness is not the same as having.

For Discussion and Reflection

- *What role do possessions play in your life?*
- *How much of what you have do you really need?*
- *What does stewardship mean to you?*

CHAPTER TEN

FRIENDS OF JESUS

We have seen that thinking Catholic is not a solitary exercise. Thinking Catholic is necessarily interpersonal and relational. One interpersonal relationship has a unique importance in the life of believers. It is our friendship with the Lord Jesus.

Some people look on Jesus only as a historical figure, a blip on the screen of the human drama, a dreamer who was put to death by his enemies because he just didn't fit in. Others look on Jesus as a great teacher, a man who told other human beings about God from his point of view and invited them to share in his ideas. Still others see Jesus as a stern lawgiver who told us what God demands of us and who promised to come back to judge each of us according to the way we listened to what he had to say.

Those who think Catholic look on Jesus primarily as a friend. Friends are those who love each other, who see the good in the other and who want to do good for the other. A friend will appreciate the good qualities of a friend and will be willing to overlook his or her limitations. Friends spend time together, not just doing things that both enjoy, but also sharing with one another what has happened since they last met—their successes and their frustrations, their dreams and their fears. Sometimes it is enough just to be in the company of our friends, without doing or saying anything at all. Friends are people who share themselves, not for any specific purpose, not for gain or profit, but simply because they are friends.

Jesus was big on friendship. He had a circle of followers who traveled with him and listened to what he had to say. He taught them as friends (see Luke 12:4). He called them his friends because he shared with them what he had come from the Father to bring to us human beings (see John 15:15). Their friendship was based on their willingness to listen to and follow what Jesus taught (see John 15:14).

When he was about to be done to death for his faithfulness to his heavenly Father, Jesus spoke about laying down his life for his friends and about how this was the greatest thing that one person could do for another (see John 15:13). And when one of his closest associates brought Jesus' enemies to where he could be arrested without resistance, Jesus nonetheless addressed him as friend (see Matthew 26:50). Jesus died for friendship.

Jesus' friendship was not limited just to this close circle of disciples. He had time for all sorts of people: for women of uncertain reputation (see Luke 7:39), for the poor and the disabled (see Mark 1:32 and following), for ordinary people who seemed to lack direction in their lives (see Matthew 9:36). He was even at ease in the company of those who were collaborating with the Roman oppressors of his people and those who weren't particularly careful about religious observance. He became notorious as "a friend of tax collectors and sinners" (see Luke 7:34).

This taste for friendship did not end with Jesus' death. After he had been raised from the dead, his first concern was to get back in touch with his friends (see Mark 16:7). He was patient with their uncertainty about who and what he was (see Luke 24:36 ff.). He explained to them the significance of what had happened to him (see Luke 24:26 and following). And with poor Peter, the boastful coward who had promised Jesus undying loyalty and then refused to admit that he even knew him, Jesus took special pains. He got Peter to acknowledge no less than three times that he still loved him, and then lovingly put him in charge of his flock. Their friendship was sealed by forgiveness (see John 21:15 ff.).

Then came the time when Jesus' earthly mission was over. He didn't say good-bye to his friends as if he were going away from them. Friends like to stay together, and Jesus' last words to his friends were, "And behold, I am with you always, until the end of the age" (Matthew 28:20). The friendship had not ended. It had merely entered a new phase.

Thinking Catholic means sharing in that friendship that Jesus promised would last to the end of time. Thinking Catholic means being friends with Jesus.

Catholics acknowledge Jesus as truly God, begotten of the Father before all ages, one with the Father and the Holy Spirit. Jesus is the Word of the Father, the expression of the Father's will for all creation, past, present and future. At the end of time, Jesus will come to judge the living and the dead and our eternal destiny depends on the degree to which we have listened to and obeyed his commands.

But with all that, Jesus is still our friend, one who knows us and loves us as we are and who wants to do good for us. Jesus wants to be our principal friend, the One with whom we are more closely associated than with anybody else. If the story of each of our lives is the story of our participation in God's celebration of goodness and love, it is also the story of our relationship with Jesus.

Relationships demand contact, and friendship with Jesus means living in his company. Thinking Catholic involves an ongoing awareness of the presence and the love of Jesus, not as a distant figure from the past, but as one near and real to us. When Jesus said he would be with his friends until the end of time, he meant that he would be with *us*. We never have to be alone, because the greatest friend we can ever have is always near.

This is not to say that everything we say and do is acceptable to Jesus. Real friendship does not call for approval when friends do something silly or harmful to themselves or to others. Friends owe it to one another to relate in truthfulness, and sometimes one friend has to say unpleasant things to the other. Our friendship with Jesus can be demanding, not because Jesus is looking for something for himself from us, but because he is looking for what is best for us.

Sometimes Jesus' friendship with us involves forgiveness, as it did with Peter. Our inherited inclination to sin and our chronic short-sightedness often bring us to abuse the friendship and the presence of Jesus. It is possible for us to go so far astray that we don't even want his friendship anymore. But that doesn't mean it's over. When we turn back to Jesus, he is there as always, assuring us that he loves us in spite of what we have done.

Who and what we are is reflected by the kinds of friends we have. Thinking Catholic means treasuring and cultivating a lifelong friendship with the One who offered his life for his friends, who went out of his way to give comfort to those in pain and who paid attention to people that everybody else had written off. Being friends with Jesus gives a special dimension to our participation in God's work of creation here and now. Being friends with Jesus now also teaches us what we have to look forward to when we come finally into God's kingdom.

Thinking Catholic means being at home with the presence of the Lord.

For Discussion and Reflection

• *Do you consider Jesus to be your friend?*
• *How do you experience the friendship of Jesus?*
• *What does Jesus ask for in friendship with you?*

CHAPTER ELEVEN

KEEPING IN TOUCH

Some people look on prayer as something like the visits to Santa Claus that children make. It's not something that happens regularly, but only at a special time. They climb upon the knee of the man in the white beard, inform him of their desires, and hope that, if they have been good enough, he will listen to them and they will get what they have asked for.

Authentic prayer isn't quite like that. It's not just asking. It's not just occasional. And getting a response doesn't depend on how good we have been. Prayer is our conscious attentiveness to the presence of our friend Jesus, of his Father, of their Spirit who dwells within us. Prayer is consciously spending time with God. Prayer is the way we keep in touch with the Lord.

There are all kinds of ways to pray. Sometimes we use formulas out of prayer books or from our memory. These formulas give us direction about how to communicate with the Lord if we're not quite sure what to say to him. If we are tired or distracted they help us focus our attention. They are useful when Christian believers pray together. Over the centuries, the psalms have been counted among the standard prayer forms for the church.

Sometimes when we pray we use our own words in a kind of formal conversation. Maybe we make a visit to the Lord in the Blessed Sacrament and just tell him how things are going with us. Maybe we thank him in the morning for the hours that lie ahead of us, or praise him in the evening for his help and presence through the day. Sometimes we need to ask the Lord for things, for help with a problem, for patience with a difficult person or for courage in suffering. Sometimes we need to apologize to the Lord when we have turned away from him or neglected him. When we pray in these ways, explicitly taking time out to chat with God, we deliberately shut out the noise of the world around us and try to give our full attention to the Lord. It's like sitting ourselves down with a friend for some serious conversation.

But there are other ways to be in touch with the Lord, more informal and casual ones. Just acknowledging the presence of Jesus when we are waiting for the traffic light to change is prayer ("Lord, I know you are with me"). So is the nod in his direction when something nice happens to us ("Thank you, Jesus!") or the quick call for help in time of urgency ("Lord, help me get there on time!"). This is the sort of prayer that I think Saint Paul had in mind when he told the early Christians to pray constantly (see 1 Thessalonians 5:17 and Ephesians 6:18).

It may well be that the depth of our attentiveness to the Lord is expressed as much by these spontaneous encounters with him as by the number of words we say out of a book or by the amount of time we spend in formal sit-down sessions—assuming that what we communicate with him in these informal ways is sincere, not just religious words we use to avoid less acceptable language. If nothing else, these quick and frequent outreaches to God insure that we don't look on God as a distant master but as a friend who is always near.

Whatever forms of prayer we may use, it is important that our prayer be balanced. Catholic thinking over the years has identified four main things that we should pray about, four contexts in which we need to be attentive to the presence of our friend, the Lord.

The most obvious, and probably the most common, is prayer of petition, when we ask God for the things we need. We tell the Lord our needs not to inform him of what we are expecting or to persuade him to give us his help. God doesn't require that of us. It's rather a matter of expressing our dependence on the Lord. Prayer of petition is one of the ways in which we acknowledge that we are God's instruments in the celebration of creation and that we can't carry out our parts properly unless he is there to help us. Prayer of petition also sensitizes us to recognize God's help when it has come to us. If we have not lifted up our needs to the Lord, we are likely to think that they have been met from some other direction.

Thanksgiving is another context in which people need to pray. Thanksgiving is always appropriate because there is always something to be thankful for: a good day, a problem resolved, an unexpected blessing. And then there are the ordinary things that those who are not attuned to prayer might take for granted: sunshine, rain, honeybees, a break in the traffic jam. Those who are really skilled in prayer can even be grateful for things that seem to be burdensome. They know that our creative and loving Father and his Son Jesus never send us anything that is exclusively bad. There is always a reason to be grateful.

Another main category of prayer is contrition. We have already seen that an awareness of our own sinfulness is a significant part of thinking Catholic. The prayer of sorrow, asking for forgiveness, is one of the ways in which we make explicit that awareness—not in order to punish ourselves or to instill a sense of worthlessness, but to remain conscious that God loves us in spite of our limitations. To neglect the prayer of contrition is either to forget that we are sinners, which is an exercise in denial, or to forget how much God loves us, which is an exercise in self-destruction.

Then there is the prayer of praise, when we simply acknowledge how good God is, how creative, how generous, how merciful, how understanding, how patient, how providential. The prayer of praise is not complimenting God so that he will remain kind to us, a sort of self-interested flattery. The prayer of praise is a way in which we keep ourselves conscious of the kind of creation in which we live and the kind of Lord who is in charge of it. God doesn't need our praise. We need to praise God so that we don't forget who and what we are, so that we remain aware of what we are here for, so that we will be ready to join in the unending chorus of praise to which God calls us in the kingdom.

Within the community of the faithful are men and women who dedicate their whole lives to prayer. They are the contemplatives, such as Trappists or Poor Clares. Their purpose is not to get away from it all and avoid the burdens of ordinary life. Rather, their purpose is to spend themselves in the highest activity of which human beings are capable, immediate and ongoing contact with God. In the process, they remind the rest of us of the purpose of prayer and keep us aware of what a wonderful and blessed thing it is to stay in touch with the Lord. They are the virtuosos and the teachers of prayer.

Prayer is not one more obligation that God has imposed on us, another chore in addition to doing good and avoiding evil. Prayer is a rich and varied exercise of conscious association with the Lord. It is a diet that keeps us strong and lively, vigorous in our execution of the part in creation that God has assigned to us, grateful for his unceasing gifts, confident in his ongoing presence. We need prayer for our spirits as much as we need food for our bodies.

The Lord is the source and goal of everything we are and of everything we aspire to. It's important for us to keep in touch. Thinking Catholic means being persons of prayer.

For Discussion and Reflection

- *How often do you pray?*
- *What do you pray about?*
- *Do you enjoy prayer?*

CHAPTER TWELVE

THE WHOLE PICTURE

The word *catholic* means whole, entire, universal. We Catholics are part of a family community that extends throughout the whole world, that teaches the entire message of Jesus and offers the entire range of gifts that Jesus intended for his followers, a community that somehow embraces the universal history of humankind. Thinking Catholic means being aware of these dimensions of our relationship with God.

But thinking Catholic also involves a particularly "catholic" way of looking at the world in general. It is an inclination to see things not as isolated phenomena in the vast complex of creation and human history, but as a single, organized plan. It is an inclination to see the parts in relation to the whole picture. There is an all-embracing perspective in thinking Catholic.

This tendency to look at the whole picture is a consequence of the Catholic Christian belief about creation. That which surrounds us in the world is not the outcome of chance happenings over millions of years, but rather the unfolding of the single program of God's desire to share his goodness and love. It all arises from a single source and is all directed toward a single purpose. It's all part of the one celebration. It all hangs together in a single fabric of consistency.

Thinking in terms of the big picture is also a consequence of the Catholic Christian belief about redemption. When God became a human being in Jesus, the whole world entered into a deeper relationship with God. The world is no longer just a product of God's creative will. It is also the place where God actually lived as a human being long ago and where God still lives today in the ongoing life of Christ. Every aspect of it has been touched by the one Redeemer, and every facet of it will be united and preserved when the Redeemer's kingdom comes in its final fullness.

When those who think Catholic look at creation and its source and purpose in this way, it is not some sort of abstract philosophical exercise. It is the expression of a mindset that seeks to grasp the fullness and the coherence of creation and redemption in order to acknowledge and praise the goodness and wisdom of the Lord. In the final analysis, the Catholic worldview is an exercise in appreciation.

In the history of Catholic thinking there are many examples of this endeavor to see the whole picture. One of the most significant is the *Summa Theologicae* (Summary of Theology) of Saint Thomas Aquinas. This "summary" runs to about 3,200 pages of small print in double columns. It is primarily concerned with the study of God: God's nature, God's plan for our salvation and the execution of that plan through redemption by Christ, God's care for us in the church, God's plans for us at the end of time. But it also deals with the meaning of creation, both visible and invisible, with human morality and the way we work as rational creatures, with prayer and vice and virtue. The *Summa* of Saint Thomas is an immense grid on which there is a place to position just about everything one could imagine, including branches of knowledge that have developed since Saint Thomas wrote. His *Summa* is one of the masterworks of thinking Catholic, but it is only one of dozens of such works that Catholic thinkers have produced.

A more modern example of looking at the whole picture is the *Catechism of the Catholic Church*, which was published in 1994. Here the church presents the fullness of its teaching as expressed in the Creed, in the sacraments, in the Ten Commandments (viewed as an expression of our life in Christ) and in the Our Father (viewed as the basic pattern for Christian prayer). It is not a collection of miscellaneous propositions or a laundry list of teachings, but rather a coherent and complete view of the way things are, organized to show that it all fits together in a single picture.

The *Catechism of the Catholic Church* does not deal with each and every conceivable bit of human knowledge, any more than Saint Thomas's *Summa* does, but, as expressions of thinking Catholic, both works provide a context in which everything fits somewhere or other. Fruit flies and supernovas, the laws of economics and of subatomic particles, the history of twelfth-century China and the poetry of Shakespeare—none of this is irrelevant to God's plan of creation and redemption. None of it is foreign to thinking Catholic. It all belongs somewhere in the big picture.

But seeing the whole picture is not something that is confined to big books. It also takes place in the ordinary life of those who think Catholic.

As believers, we know that each one of us has been called to further God's purposes and that each of us fits somewhere in God's plan. None of us is unimportant or expendable. Similarly, the events of our lives, sad ones and happy ones, all make their contribution to what God has in mind for us. Nothing happens by chance. Even sins can be turned to a good purpose by our almighty Father. And those parts of our lives that we simply can't understand are not for that reason outside the big picture. They are simply signs that God's ways are not our ways. Christian faith in divine providence involves an awareness that there is one carefully planned scheme of things, that we are part of that scheme and that all creation is somehow connected with us in bringing it to completion.

This concern with the whole picture is one of the driving forces of Catholic education. Learning about our faith is not just a matter of "religion" and "morality." It also involves learning the what and the why of creation as a whole. Nothing is foreign to Catholic education simply because nothing is foreign to us—or to God.

The world around us is often suspicious of big pictures. Some hold that there is no one big picture. Others believe that, if there is, it is so far beyond our understanding that it is irrelevant to us. The culture in which we live is much more comfortable with a narrow focus, a focus that is directed principally to me, to my needs, to my wants. The rest of humankind is of no concern to me. The rest of creation is only meaningful to the extent that it is useful to me.

Such a narrow focus is unfortunate because it excludes so much understanding, goodness, beauty and joy. People who see things this way prefer to spend their lives picking over the hors d'oeuvres instead of sitting down at the main table with the other guests at the celebration.

Thinking Catholic means being concerned with the whole picture, because the whole picture is the context in which we are called to be and to live. Ever since creation and, even more, ever since the Son of God became part of creation as a human being, there is no aspect of what is that is alien to God and to God's family. The interior life of God, Father and Son and Holy Spirit, God's goodness and love, God's mercy, God's plan, human history from beginning to end, human society, human health, human achievement in the arts, the realms of animals and plants and minerals, the vast sweep of the skies whose extent we are just beginning to learn: It's all part of the picture that God wants us to understand and appreciate and enjoy. Thinking Catholic means thinking big. It means thinking universal.

For Discussion and Reflection

- *What aspects of creation are most appealing to you?*
- *How have you experienced God's providence in your life?*
- *What relationship do you see between education and faith?*

CHAPTER THIRTEEN

CALLED INTO CHRIST TOGETHER

The Catholic Church means different things to different people. To some who are not its members the Catholic Church is the anti-Christ, a usurper that proclaims false teaching about Jesus. To others the Catholic Church is an interesting historical curiosity, a remnant of the past whose contemporary significance is confined to offering contrast to more enlightened modern ways of thinking. To others the church is just one more religious organization put together by people who happen to share the same set of beliefs.

Even Catholics have different ways of looking at the church, depending on which aspects of it they choose to emphasize. Most Catholics look at the church with affection as a community in which they find comfort. Some look at the church with anger because of what they have suffered at the hands of its representatives. Some like to concentrate on the church around us as the church militant, valiantly struggling to be faithful to the Lord and to defend itself against its enemies as it moves forward to its final triumph. Some like to view the church as a preacher of social justice or as a stern teacher of unchanging doctrine. Some use images when they think of the church: the people of God, the flock of Christ, the holy mother, the field full of good grain interspersed with weeds. All these ways of looking on the church have some merit, because the church is, in fact, complex: a collection of saints and sinners, a fabric of successes and failures, a reality too intricate to be fully expressed by a single image or a single idea.

Certain elements, however, must be included in any adequate grasp of the church. First of all, the church is about Christ. It is the continuation of the life and mission of the Lord Jesus. Next, the church is composed of people who have been called to it by the Lord.

The church is not an organization put together by human beings to preserve the memory and the teaching of Jesus, but a gathering of men and women who have been called by God through baptism to participate in the ongoing life of Christ. Finally, the church is not a collection of individuals, each relating to the Lord on a one-to-one basis, but a community of believers interacting with each other and with Christ in the context of the world. The church is the body of those called into Christ together.

There is no denying that there are problems and limitations in the church. Not all those who are called into Christ together are faithful to their calling. Not all those who speak and act in the name of the church are everything they should be. The church reflects the constraints of human history, so that some things the church did in the past now seem inappropriate from the perspective of the present. But all this, real as it is, is merely static in the church's transmission of its message.

Thinking Catholic involves acknowledging and accepting the church in its full reality.

In and through the church Christ makes us holy in his Spirit. Every stage of life is touched by the love and the life of the Lord through his sacraments: baptism that gives us birth, confirmation and the Eucharist that offer us maturity and strength, reconciliation and the anointing of the sick that deal with our moral and physical weaknesses. It's all part of God's plan to make us holy as Christ is holy.

In and through the church Christ teaches us. Christ teaches us about the world and our part in it, about the significance of our life, about the Father's love for us, about what the Father has in store for us when our earthly life is over. Christ teaches us about the worth and dignity of other people and about the dangers of getting too involved with what surrounds us. Christ teaches us that, in the last analysis, he is the unifying power that brings everything together into one and gives significance to all that is.

And all this happens in the context of our togetherness in him. Christ makes us holy through the agency of his ordained priests. Christ teaches us in the context of our families, miniature churches established by the sacrament of matrimony, and then through other teachers who speak in his name. Christ sanctifies, teaches and cares for us through others in less formal ways, too. The love that believers show to other people is the love of Christ. The example of dedication, commitment, sacrifice and prayer that believers offer to those around them is not pious posturing but the simple expression of what friendship with Christ is all about. We need each other because it is in each other that we encounter the Lord. And unless we encounter the Lord, our lives are without meaning.

The church has been around for a long time, and so we have an extended and rich family history. It includes those members we call saints (starting with Mary, the mother of Jesus) who have been conspicuously faithful and generous in their response to the Lord's call. It also includes other members of whom we are less proud.

Our family history includes official rituals and personal devotional practices, some dating from the times of the apostles, some from the imperial court of Byzantium, some from the Middle Ages, some from just a few years ago. Every era of the church makes its contribution to the way in which we express the relationship that Christ has established with us.

Our family history includes a highly articulated body of teaching that reflects, clarifies and develops the teaching of Christ as it has been received and applied over the centuries. It involves thinkers and scholars such as Augustine and Dante and Newman, Julian of Norwich and Teresa of Avila, who have shared with the church their insights about God, about the order of the world, about prayer, about what it means to be a friend of Jesus. Each has made the riches of Christ available to the community of the faithful in his or her particular way.

It's all part of the church, yet it all reflects the same basic reality of being called into Christ together.

The church expresses its nature most eloquently in the Sunday celebration of the Eucharist. Here is a gathering of people who have been reborn into the life of Christ. Some are fervent believers. Some are lukewarm. Some aren't sure why they are there at all. Yet they are together in the Lord. And at their gathering, they hear the call of the Lord as the Lord offers it to them in sacred Scripture and as it is applied to the here and now by the Lord's priest. They express their acceptance of the Lord's teaching in psalms and hymns. Then they offer themselves to their heavenly Father in conjunction with the offering of faithfulness that Christ made on the cross. In response to their offering, Christ gives them himself in Holy Communion to deepen his life in them and to strengthen them to carry that life with them into the often crazy world in which they live.

For those who think Catholic, Sunday Mass is not just an obligation to be fulfilled. It is a gift, an opportunity to be in touch with the Lord and to be in touch with one another. It is a source of light and energy and joy. It's something we need in order to stay aware that the real worth of our life consists in being called into Christ together.

The church is old and new, comforting and frustrating, demanding and reassuring. The Lord calls us to embrace it all. Thinking Catholic means being in love with the church.

For Discussion and Reflection

• *What is your attitude toward the church?*
• *Which saints are your favorites? Why?*
• *Do you look forward to Sunday Mass? Why? Why not?*

CHAPTER FOURTEEN

LEARNING

Learning is something we do all the time. Recently some people I was with were talking about our public schools. One person said that it's wrong to blame the schools for all the difficulties of our society because the schools have access to the students for only about six hours a day for one hundred and eighty days a year. They teach as well as they can, but for all the other hours of the day and for all the other days of the year the students are being taught—and are learning—elsewhere. They learn from television, from their friends, from what they see and hear on the streets in their neighborhoods. Schools provide only some of the learning. Most of what students learn comes from elsewhere.

It's the same for the rest of us. We are all being taught and we are all learning all sorts of things all the time.

We all need to learn because practically nothing of what we need to know in order to live and function as human beings is instinctive. Most of this knowledge is acquired. Some is acquired unconsciously, as when we learn to speak our native language by listening and practicing at home as we grow up. Some is acquired consciously, as when we learn to ride a bicycle or use a computer. But learn we must.

It's no different with thinking Catholic. It's not something that comes to us automatically. We have to learn it.

The foundations of thinking Catholic come to many of us in our families. If we are lucky enough to be born into a family of those who think Catholic, we learn the fundamental lessons from our parents and our brothers and sisters. Our basic attitudes about the world, about God, about prayer, about the meaning of effort and suffering, about success and failure, about possessions, about the church all come to us through our families. We learn most of these lessons unconsciously, just by watching and listening to those around us. But all these attitudes are learned, and somebody has to teach them to us.

As we grow toward maturity, what we have learned in our families is both supplemented and tested by the wider world. We go to school. We make friends and find activities outside our family. Eventually we get a job. Eventually we are on our own. In all these circumstances, we are learning. And what we are learning either strengthens or weakens what we learned at home.

But as we launch into individual independence, new challenges arise, new sets of circumstances that are different from what we may have known before. They may have to do with our work or with our personal relationships or with our ambitions. For most people, starting a family of their own presents whole new vistas of the unknown that have to be dealt with. And we have to learn how to deal with all these things. Our previous experiences, at home and elsewhere, may have taught us the principles, but now we are faced with how to apply the principles to these specific circumstances. We always need to learn.

And the learning never ends. Each stage of our lives presents new questions, new demands for learning. Some people who do well in school do not do well at their jobs. Some people who seem very successful in youth and middle age find themselves at a loss when old age sets in.

If we have learned the fundamentals of thinking Catholic at home, we at least have a foundation to build on. If we have not, then the task of acquiring sane and sound attitudes toward the world and the Lord and the meaning of our human life is more demanding. But, whatever our personal circumstances, thinking Catholic is something that has to be learned and something that we have to keep learning throughout our whole lives.

Thinking Catholic presupposes a certain fund of informational knowledge, truths about our heavenly Father and Jesus and the church and the world and standards of behavior. But that's not enough. If we don't go beyond that, our faith will become irrelevant to what goes on in our lives day by day. Merely "knowing" that God loves us won't make much difference if we are unable to see what that means when we fail an exam or lose our job or get a promotion or fall in love with somebody.

In addition to basic information, thinking Catholic involves attitudes and habits, and these attitudes and habits have to be learned and practiced.

Probably everyone who thinks Catholic would give his or her own list of attitudes and habits that contribute to maintaining faithfulness and sanity in the course of our lifetime. The little list that follows offers some of the things that I have found important in my own life.

Looking for the Lord. The handiwork of the creator is everywhere. The love of the Lord Jesus is everywhere. The action of the Spirit is everywhere. But we have to learn to see it, and in order to see it we have to become accustomed to looking for it. Those who think Catholic try to be attentive to the presence and action of God in every aspect of their lives—in the successes and the failures, in the joys and the sorrows. Whatever is going on, they ask themselves, "Where is the Lord in this?"

Responding to the Lord. God does not call on us to be spectators in our lives. We are participants, and in order to participate appropriately in our lives we have to respond to what the Lord asks of us. Thinking Catholic means looking at the circumstances in which we find ourselves—our individual circumstances and the larger circumstances of the world around us—and asking ourselves, "What does the Lord look for from me here and now?"

Being grateful to the Lord. If we are aware that the loving Lord is the principal actor in our lives and that the Lord is interested in us and in our world, then we will necessarily be inclined to thank the Lord. Somehow or another, God is always blessing us. Somehow or another, gratitude is always appropriate. "What can I thank the Lord for now?"

Nourishing the life of the Lord in us. Life involves the expenditure of energy, and energy needs to be replaced. We can't live our whole lives on the fund of faith and practice that we may have received in our childhood. We have to keep replenishing the fuel supply. This means a lifetime of learning about the Lord through Scripture and the teaching of the church. It means regular participation in the celebration of the sacraments. It means consistent contact with other persons of faith. Our society is big on following a healthy diet. Thinking Catholic means being attentive to getting proper spiritual nourishment.

All this could be reduced to two basic requirements for thinking Catholic: reflection and prayer. Reflection means consciously looking at our lives from the perspective of the Lord. Reflection is particularly important in our time because there is so much noise and glitter in the world around us that we can easily lose track of what's important unless we are accustomed to looking beneath it all for the reality that lies at the heart of things. Prayer means lifting our selves and our lives and our brothers and sisters and our world up to the Lord, maintaining constant contact with the sources of meaning and energy.

None of this is automatic. None of it can be taken care of once and for all. Thinking Catholic is a habit, and habits are acquired by practice, by doing things over and over again, day after day, until they become second nature to us, and then continuing the practice so that the habits don't gradually get replaced by other less healthy ones.

Thinking Catholic is based on gifts that God gives each of us. But it is also based on our own decisions and practice. It is something that has to be worked at and learned.

Learning goes on our whole life long, consciously or unconsciously. And if we are not learning to think Catholic, then we are learning something else.

For Discussion and Reflection

- *Do you have regular times for reflection?*
- *How and when do you pray?*
- *Is learning part of your life?*

CONCLUSION

We live in a crazy world. It is a world that makes promises of happiness that it can never deliver, a world in which many look on human life as a commodity to be used rather than a gift to be respected, a world that denies the reality of evil, a world in which the principal virtue is selfishness. It is a world that cannot look much beyond the here and now, a world that can find meaning only in the satisfaction of immediate wants and needs. It's a crazy world. The craziness is all around us. There's no avoiding contact with it. Yet this is the world in which we are called to live.

The only way to avoid being infected by the craziness is to have different values and different goals—healthy, true and realistic ones, consciously and firmly held. What's needed is a whole different mindset, a fundamentally different way of approaching the challenges and opportunities of each day. Anything less than that will not be enough to keep us faithful to what God has called us to be.

In this last section I have described some of the many aspects of such a mindset, which I have called "thinking Catholic." Another writer might have made a different selection or provided a different order of presentation. But all aspects of thinking Catholic have a common ground. When all is said and done, thinking Catholic means having faith.

In this context, "faith" is not a series of propositions we accept with our minds. Nor is it a kind of mindless assumption that somehow everything is going to turn out all right. It is rather an understanding of and a response to the way things really are, an understanding that involves deeply held convictions, a response that includes the gift of our very selves to an adventure whose origins and goals are beyond our own making.

Thinking Catholic means accepting what God has told us about himself and about us, that whole complex of revelation offered by Jesus and proclaimed by his church. But what we accept is not merely intellectual information, as when we accept what the experts tell us about ancient history or the inner workings of the atom. What God offers us is not just interesting information but basic truth about who and what we are, where we have come from and where we are headed, truth about the significance of our corporate human past and about the value of every moment of the present—basic truth that helps us make sense of literally everything. God doesn't offer us only knowledge. God offers us meaning, and it is meaning that makes the difference between wisdom and madness.

Because what God offers us is not mere information, we cannot assimilate it with simple assent. For example, "I believe that there are three Persons in God" and "I believe that the Battle of Waterloo took place in 1815" are not the same kind of material. Merely "knowing" what God reveals to us is not enough. We have to make it our own. We have to understand the significance of what God is teaching us.

This understanding that God offers us is not one more program that we can tune in to as we surf our way through life. It is something different and deeper, and it calls for a special kind of attention. Moreover, it is so rich and complex that in a whole lifetime of attentiveness we can only begin to grasp it. The conviction that accompanies real faith demands practice in looking for the Lord. It requires a consciously acquired habit of mindfulness. Meaning does not come easily.

But faith is more than understanding. It is also response. It means giving our hearts and minds to participation in the project for which God made the world, the project in which God has called us to collaborate. The response involves gratitude as we become ever more aware of God's presence and action in our lives. It involves patience as we try to tease out the significance of what is going on around us. It involves the joyful gift of our talents and our resources in executing the role that God has assigned to us. Above all, it involves love, the will to give back to God in proportion as God has given to us.

Like the discovery of meaning, the response to meaning also requires practice—a whole lifetime of it. As we grow in our awareness of the meaning of the Lord in our world and in our lives, we keep finding new ways, deeper ways, often more demanding ways in which to respond. Our response is much more than keeping a set of rules. It is rather learning to act consistently with who and what we are. As our awareness of who and what we are matures, so does our response.

Faith involves understanding and response, deliberately pursued and consistently practiced. That's the agenda that God has given us for our lives.

Just as our lives are God's gift to us, so is our faith. Left to ourselves, we have no way in which to find meaning in the apparent jumble of the world around us. Left to ourselves, we can make no fitting response. Just as it is the Lord who provides the revelation, so it is the Lord who enables us to grasp it and to answer it. Everything is gift.

To have and to practice faith, to understand the world and its meaning and our part in it, to grasp the value of my human life and of every human life, to be aware of the presence of God in what goes on within us and around us, to savor our relationship with Jesus and with the brothers and sisters of Jesus in the church, to see how it all fits together in a coherent vision, to accept it joyfully and confidently as God's gift and plan for us, to respond to it all with love on our part even as it is offered with love on God's part: That's what thinking Catholic is all about.

A long time ago, soon after the church began, Saint Paul wrote a letter to the Christians of Rome. It's a long and complicated letter, basically concerned with the meaning of faith. Toward the end of the letter is a long section about putting faith into practice. At the beginning of that section, Saint Paul urges his readers: "Do not conform yourself to this age but be transformed by the renewal of your mind, that you may discern what is the will of God, what is good and pleasing and perfect" (Romans 12:2). This summons is also addressed to us.

Faithfulness in a crazy world is not easy. It never has been. It is not something that follows automatically from being a member of the church or from knowing church teaching. The renewal of our mind to which Saint Paul invites us requires attention and effort.

Yet faithfulness is not just an ongoing struggle against heavy odds. It is an enterprise of eager confidence. We are called to live in an awareness of the profound meaning that God has put into his creation and to respond energetically and enthusiastically to that meaning with the resources that God has bestowed on us so generously. We are called to deal with things the way they really are. That's what constitutes faithfulness. That's what constitutes sanity. That's thinking Catholic.

For Discussion and Reflection

- *Is there meaning in your life?*
- *How do you respond to the Lord in your life?*
- *Do you have and practice faith?*

INDEX

Abba, 30, 41
abortion, 173, 189, 191
absolution, 99, 101–102
abstinence, 117
Act of Contrition, 106
Advent, 95, 102
affection, 180
almsgiving, during Lent, 118
Angelus, 108
anointing of sick, 59–60. *See also* "last
    rites"
    Holy Communion and, 160
    multi-purpose of, 159–160
    sacrament of reconciliation and, 160
Anthony, 147
apostles, 39, 42, 60, 71
    awakening of, 43
    Holy Spirit and, 65
    understanding of, 72
appreciation, 222
Aquinas, Thomas, 105, 222–223
Arians, 43
artificial contraception, 189
artists, 14
Ash Wednesday, 117
assisted suicide, 189
Assumption of Mary, 96

baptism
    acceptance of, 167
    as "constitutional" sacrament, 59
    as essential beginning, 130
    grace and, 54
    problems with, 129
beliefs, 5
    Catholic Christian, 221
believers, 5, 153
    agenda, for lives of, 66
    blessings and, 165–166
    life of, 154
    priorities of, 154
benediction, 112
Bible, 187
Blessed Sacrament, visiting, 111–115

blessings, 78
    believers and, 165–166
Body/ Blood of Christ, 68
    church as, 187
Book of Genesis, 11–12, 178
boredom, 20
Brideshead Revisited (Waugh), 6, 114
burial, 161

Camus, Albert, 20
candles. *See* vigil candles
canonization, 149
Catechism of the Catholic Church, viii, 3,
    93, 101, 175, 222–223
catholic, 221
Catholic Christian beliefs, 221
Catholic heart/mind, 175
Catholic practices, vii
    intensity of, 167
    principles of, 165
    sacraments as, 166
    styles of, 167
Catholic schools, 131
"Catholic things," 154
Catholic thinking, 174–175, 179,
    184–185, 192
    attitudes of, 231–232
    faith and, 235
    family and, 205
    foundation of, 229
    life of Christ and, 196
    love of church and, 228
    perspective in, 199
    sin and, 202–203
    as universal, 224
    viewing evil and, 194
Catholic worldview, 222
Catholicism, 89
charity, 6
children, 205
    education of, 130–131
    faith and, 130
    marriage and, 126
    raising Catholic, 129–133, 166